PRAISE FOR *TRIBAL ABUNDANCE*

"Ildi's story is one for all of us. ... *Tribal Abundance* is an easy read, a great conversation starter, and a solid reminder that most of our significant accomplishments and experiences happen when we're in connection."

—Ed Muzio, Best-selling author of
Iterate: Run a Fast, Flexible, Focused Management Team

"Ildikó...defines 'the new normal' in a way you can find your place, your connection and your community. She finds a way to make it safe to face your fears and feel a sense of belonging and connection."

—Kim Nugent, Ed.D., CEO and best-selling author of
*Promotion Protocol: Unlock the Secrets of
Promotability & Career Success*

"Compassionate, with boundless talent and enthusiasm, Ildikó Oravecz has shared her essence with a much larger world. Now, more will know about her and see how courageously she shares her life with others."

—Nancy Mills, Founder, *TheSpiritedWoman.com*

"Ildikó Oravecz is the embodiment of Tribal Abundance. Nothing demonstrates this better than a recent encounter where a coach in Ildi's immediate space sought accreditation in a motivational tool that Ildi uses widely and often differentiates her work, called PRINT®. When asked if she was comfortable with the prospect, her response was, 'more PRINT® coaches = more awareness of PRINT® = more folks wanting PRINT® = more work and business for ALL of us.' Unlike the zero-sum mentality that many exhibit, Ildi's courage, positivity, and trust are exemplary and invigorating. I can testify firsthand, she practices what she preaches. She is a shining example of the fulfillment and success attainable when one lives by the principles of Tribal Abundance."

—Dr. Paul Hertz, President, The Paul Hertz Group,
Co-Creator of PRINT®

"Ildi offers up a full plate of delightful stories and reflective experiences, and then finds a way to anchor them to a practical roadmap for leading a more beautiful life… a must-read for tapping into your own abundant heart."

—Katie K. Snapp, Founder, Skirt Strategies: Training
and Encouragement for Women in Leadership

"From the heart of a little girl to the depths of a grown woman, Ildikó Oravecz sheds light on the power of connection, the roots of segregation, and the impact of both in our lives. She reveals the art of finding one's tribe, one's sense of community, and one's authentic self."

—Chloe Rachel Gallaway, Author of
The Soulful Child: Twelve Years in the Wilderness

"If you have ever struggled with feeling like there is 'not enough,' then this is the book for you. ...This book will guide you towards the understanding that there is always more than enough. ... It is Ildikó Oravecz's way of sharing her gift with others so they too can feel connected and find their place in the world."

—Yvonne Williams Casaus, Registered Play Therapist and best-selling author of *A Drop of Water: A Spiritual Journey*

Denise –
You must be an amazing
person to have Mia in
your tribe! Enjoy!
Helen

Denise,
Happy Birthday!!
My friend, wrote
this book.
I thought you

TRIBAL ABUNDANCE

Living Courageously in an Uncertain World

would it.
enjoy

♡, Mia
xoxox

TRIBAL ABUNDANCE

Living Courageously in an Uncertain World

ILDIKÓ ORAVECZ

Copyright © 2019 by Ildikó Oravecz. All rights reserved. Printed in the United States of America. No part of this book may be used or reproduced in any manner whatsoever without written permission except in the case of brief quotations included in critical articles and reviews. For information, address Permissions@CitrinePublishing.com. To contact the author, visit www.HighPerformanceConsulting.com or www.TribalAbundance.com.

Limit of Liability/Disclaimer of Warranty: While the publisher and author have used their best efforts in preparing this book, they make no representations or warranties with respect to the accuracy or completeness of the contents of this book and specifically disclaim any implied warranties of merchantability or fitness for a particular purpose. The author of this book does not dispense medical advice or prescribe the use of any technique as a form of treatment for physical, emotional, or medical problems without the advice of a physician. The intent of the author is only to offer information of a general nature to help you in your quest for well-being. In the event you use any of the information in the book for yourself, which is your constitutional right, the author and publisher assume no responsibility for your actions. The views expressed in this work are solely those of the author and do not necessarily reflect the views of the publisher.

Cover Design by Lila Romero • *Author Photo by Sarah Crichlow, sarahstella.com*

Library of Congress Cataloging-in-Publication Data

Oravecz, Ildikó
Tribal Abundance: Living Courageously in an Uncertain World

p. cm.

Paperback ISBN: 978-1-947708-72-3
Ebook ISBN: 978-1-947708-74-7
Library of Congress Control Number: 2019932435
First Edition, February 2019

Ⓒ CITRINE PUBLISHING
Asheville, NC, USA
(828) 585 - 7030
www.CitrinePublishing.com

To my first tribe, my parents

CONTENTS

THE PRACTICE

FOREWORD

With great opportunity comes fear. And so it is for the human being, standing soaked in a cloak of toxicity...waiting for the cleanse of abundance to find us.

Having not known what it was like to truly be accepted and feel close to friends, I ran like a frightened child when the opportunity to connect with others presented itself. I pretended to connect. I smiled, I nodded. I had many friends...and I kept them all at arm's length. All of them. Yes, this was fine. This was safe. But if you asked me to go deeper, I froze. I simply didn't know how to connect with people, and the fear of learning was so great that it was easier to let the opportunity pass me by. Stuck in a fog of illusion, I didn't know what it meant to move. This was my life.

This picture changed for me in 2012. They say we all have a threshold that, when crossed, changes everything. I was standing just past that line. Having lost my closest ally, my only sibling, Tina, to sepsis two years prior, I had only a handful of relationships in which I felt comfortable enough to relax and let down my guard (and I was either married to the person or related by blood). I could no longer survive in this gated world that I had built for myself. Something had to change. And so, feeling sheer terror, I did the opposite of what I was conditioned to do. I closed my eyes and I moved. I walked into a world that was totally foreign to me. I dove head first into a world of deep connection.

Seven years have passed since then and so much has changed. It's a good thing we can only see the next two-hundred feet of our journey, because courageous living is a scary ride. I've fallen more times than I can count. I've embarrassed myself. I've made a lot of mistakes. And still people come. They come not in spite of my imperfections, but to my surprise, more likely because of them. They come because a true family—or as Ildikó calls it, a tribe—attracts authentic people. People who understand abundance comes in many forms. People who are grateful for life and all the parts of it. People who own their perfect imperfections like a badge of honor and pride. The more you show yourself as you truly are, the more you receive. It took me a long time to learn that lesson. Once you learn it, there's no going back.

What I can tell you is that every single moment has been worth it. The rough moments, the times I wanted to run back to the safety of disconnection, the times I fell face first…they all changed my life. If you are courageous enough to find a truly authentic and abundant-minded tribe, yours will most certainly change too.

Part of my journey to finding my tribe included meeting Ildikó in 2016. The first time we shook hands, I stared in amazement as her eyes smiled brighter than her teeth. At that moment, I knew she was going to be an important part of my life. Ildi is special in so many ways and one of them is that she gets the term "tribe" on a different level. She not only gets it, she lives it. Ildi speaks with integrity, with honesty, and with kindness. She brings people together and while connecting others, she also connects people to herself. A perfect circle of abundance.

I have seen Ildi change so many lives. I know her presence in my life has certainly changed mine. I am excited for you as you begin this incredible journey with her in this crash course of how Tribal Abundance® can change your life, both professionally and personally.

I feel certain that if you stay open and are courageous enough to raise the standard of what you will accept from your tribe, that your circle, your dreams, your confidence, and your connection to the world will explode in a direction you never dreamt possible. It's time to go there and this book can help you make your move. Walk courageously, walk optimistically, walk confidently into abundance. I applaud you.

With respect and gratitude,

Shannon Crotty
Founder/CEO Polka Dot Powerhouse

PREFACE

The Tribal Abundance® concept was something that was birthed over many years of experience. The idea of having an abundance-based mindset is not new, but the way I have put together ideas and actions into a cohesive plan certainly is. My desire is that, in reading this book, your mind is opened to the possibilities of living life in a different way.

I have included some examples from many different times in my life along with the foundational principles and structure of the Tribal Abundance® program. This is a very personal journey for me as I believe we are integrated beings who don't split into a work self and a personal life self. Rather, we "are who we are" whether we are at work, at home, or anywhere else. And so, as you read, you'll see the overlaps between my personal experiences and work/client examples, as well as learnings and summaries from some of my favorite books.

The most recent *Gallup State of the American Workplace Report* (2017) provides valuable insight into how engaged (or not) employees are at work. Over half of American workers are not engaged, while 16% are actively disengaged and miserable; only one-third (33%!) of workers are engaged. We don't want to be unhappy and disengaged at work: we don't want the drama, negative conflict, miscommunication, or turmoil. Imagine if you loved going to work and you felt connected and fulfilled there. How would that impact your life?

My hope is that by taking a Tribal Abundance® approach you will find the freedom to be authentically you, especially in your work teams, in which so many people (about 67% of you!) are unhappy and miserable. Essentially, I hope that when people like you embrace the Tribal Abundance® concepts and ideas, those statistics will flip around.

Tribal Abundance® is a registered trademark but to enhance your reading experience during the rest of this book, the trademark symbol has been left off.

INTRODUCTION

Lucy

I can feel the warmth of the sun on my back as I sit outside, cross-legged, in the grassy backyard. I can smell the rich soil and hear the leaves being tickled by the wind. I sit with my friend Lucy and we play together, enjoying each other's company with complete abandon, like only children can.

I first saw Lucy through the wire fence that separated our houses. Lush green plants lined both sides of the fence, covering the wire, but we could still peer through. I saw her bright eyes and big smile and observed that we were about the same height and build. Without understanding how I could be aware of it, I knew that we were about the same age: six years old. It felt thrilling to talk to each other through the fence, yet my little-girl heart yearned to reach out to connect beyond our words. We began a friendship through that fence, two little human beings finding a connection, and that's how I ended up inviting Lucy over to play with me.

Lucy and I spent many afternoons playing in my yard, on the days that she would visit her mother. I didn't quite understand why she didn't live with her mother, but at our age it didn't seem to matter. We often played in the sandbox, giggling as we poured sand on one another and created mud pies. One time, we had been chatting about little-girl things when the topic of my birthday party came up, and I just *knew* I wanted Lucy there. It was natural to invite her to join my party. How wonderful it would be!

The day of my party finally arrived and I could hardly believe it. I ran up and down the living room, flying my arms out like I was a kite. A twirling, churning, almost explosive feeling of joy bubbled up inside me as my guests arrived. We played games, and cake and presents abounded. I felt happy and excited as we all ran and shouted and played with abandon. But suddenly, I noticed that something had shifted, something had changed; it was as though a dark cloud of unhappiness had filled the room.

I looked up and saw that my parents were calling to me, both with that "you've done something wrong" look on their faces. My father's somber voice struck a chord of fear in me as I followed them into another room.

"Did you invite Lucy to your party?" my father asked.

"Yeeees," I responded hesitantly.

Lucy's mother was there, but no Lucy. I hadn't seen Lucy at the party. I had forgotten about the invitation, caught up as I was in all the celebration and fun and birthday frenzy. But as I stood among the adults, something felt wrong, very wrong.

"Lucy's crying and upset because you told her she could come to your party," my father said. "She can't come to your party."

I felt hot with shame and embarrassment and my face flushed bright red. My throat was dry and my heart beat faster and faster, as if a small bird had inadvertently flown inside and was flying frantically around, desperate to escape. My limbs grew hot, then cold, with shame. My mouth felt completely dry, as though my tongue was stuck to the roof of my mouth. I blinked rapidly to keep myself from crying, still not understanding what it was that I had done to get in trouble on my birthday.

I looked at my parents expectantly. I was waiting for them to explain what had happened, for them to say those magical words that adults use to make sense of everything, to make it okay.

Slowly, I came to understand that Lucy couldn't come to the party because she was black. She was the daughter of the maid who worked next door and I shouldn't have invited her. It was wrong of me to do so, and now Lucy was crying and sad.

Feelings of confusion filled me. *Lucy was my friend. We played together. We talked to each other through the fence. Why was that wrong?* Something in me yearned to scream out, to shout, "Lucy is my friend!" A powerful feeling rose up in me. It all felt so wrong not to allow Lucy to come over and yet the trusted adults in my life were telling me that *I was* wrong. That I had done something bad. I couldn't make sense of it all.

Shame and pain shattered inside me. Lucy and I never played together again.

***

As little girls do, I grew up. My Lucy Moment is a memory that has stuck with me. I'll never forget the feelings of shame, embarrassment, and the underlying sense of injustice I felt. I believe we all have Lucy Moments and the resulting emotions that surface from these moments are powerful. This Lucy Moment has stayed with me my whole life and it is as though Lucy has always been with me.

Looking back, I can only imagine what Lucy's mother must have felt. I was so focused on my parents and my feelings of shame that I didn't register what she must have been going through at the time. How heartbreaking to have to explain to your child that she couldn't go to a birthday party because of the color of her skin. And perhaps even worse, "The little girl that you've been playing with isn't really supposed to be your friend."

It wasn't until many years later that I understood that the white skin I wore protected me; it was armor against the prejudice, hate, and fear of apartheid-era South Africa. I was protected because I was white. I didn't recognize this until many years later because it just *was*. And ironically, the color of my skin was something I wanted to change when I was younger—I wanted to have the beautiful olive-colored skin all my cousins had.

For those growing up during that time in South Africa, this story is probably not uncommon. And the memory of that experience has surfaced at times when my feelings have been similar, when I've felt shame and embarrassment. What I've learned over the years is that I'm not alone. We've all had our Lucy Moments, those times when we feel as though a great injustice has been done, when we feel powerless and helpless, when we feel betrayed. And when we have those moments it's really difficult to know how to act or what to think.

It's how we respond to our Lucy Moments that determines the path of our life journey. And my Lucy Moment helped to shape me into the woman I am today, a woman I'm proud of and, I hope, a woman that Lucy would have been proud of too.

I'd like you to join me on a journey, to come along as I share other Lucy Moments I've had and how they shaped and molded me. My journey led me to a Tribal Abundance mindset and it's something I'd like to share with you. The philosophy of Tribal Abundance has been my North Star, my compass. Living in Tribal Abundance has helped me to navigate the uncertain waters of life with optimism and a sense of joy.

THE PRINCIPLES

CHAPTER 1

Loneliness Is Not the Same as Being Alone

"Loneliness and the feeling of being unwanted
is the most terrible poverty."

—*Mother Teresa*

As I peered through the bars on my crib I could see the room beyond. Sunlight was dim, fading, as the day became dusk. I was in my parents' bedroom and I could see their tall wardrobe, a deep brown wood, on the other side of the room, far away from me. In the distance I could hear voices, laughter. The urge to be with others was strong and I opened my mouth and called to them. *Will they hear me? I don't want to be alone.* My mother walked into the room—she was young, slim, beautiful. She wore a colorful dress. I firmly gripped the bars as I stood in my crib and then I stretched towards her. I wanted to be with the laughter and voices. My mother didn't touch me, yet she looked at me. Gentle murmurs came from her lips to comfort me and then she walked out of the room. I was alone again.

Even at that young age I knew that being alone was not good for me and I yearned for connection. Needing connection with others is part of the very core of our beings, in our DNA perhaps, and guides us towards our fellow human beings. This desire for connection has been the foundation upon which I've built my life.

There's a big difference between being alone and being lonely. People who are introverts have a rich inner world of thoughts and are energized when they are alone. Extroverts have a rich outer world of relationships and are energized by being with others. We're all born with a natural preference on the spectrum of introversion-extroversion and it just so happens I am an extrovert born into a mainly introvert family.

I became very comfortable being alone because that was part of my family's dynamic, yet at the same time it propelled me to be where other people were, to be with others who did not want to be alone. As that toddler in the crib, I simply wanted to *not* be alone but could not communicate that need because my language skills had not yet developed. Putting my arms out and reaching for her, crying, was still not enough to change my mother's behavior as I yearned to communicate, "I don't want to be alone!"

***

My mother, my older brother, and I walked into the tall building. It was a sunny, beautiful day and there was a sense of excitement because we were going to see the doctor. I liked Dr. Jammy; he gave us lollipops at the end of each visit and he had a deep voice that thrilled me.

We walked through the light-filled building and arrived at the lifts. I knew that we had to press a button, the doors would open, and we would walk into the lift. And then we would be magically transported.

As I looked up, I could see lights and buttons and the shiny metal doors. It was wonderful and exciting and I couldn't wait, so when the doors opened, I rushed in. When I finally turned around, I saw the doors closing on my mother's anxious face. And then she was gone.

I burst into tears.

Coming to the realization that I was alone, and lost, my little-girl heart broke. I couldn't stop the tears or the sad wailing sound coming from me. That natural liveliness I had as young girl had caused me to rush ahead with abandon, joyfully embracing all that came my way. And yet when I felt alone, I was devastated.

Then, suddenly, I realized I was not alone; there was an older gentleman on the elevator with me who firmly took my hand in his and eventually led me back to my family. At the time, there was no way I could know that learning to be alone and knowing when to reach out to others would be important in my life. But when I think back upon that moment now, that was exactly what I learned that day.

As I've mentioned, being alone doesn't necessarily mean that you're lonely, but no matter whether you're someone who craves solitude or you're someone who loves to be surrounded by people, we all desire connection. It's part of who we are as human beings and the longing to be with others is within all of us.

These early memories of feeling alone sparked in me the desire to NOT be alone, to be around others, to be surrounded. And so, a yearning was born in my heart for connection and for belonging. Both the toddler in the crib and the little lost girl who rushed into the lift displayed this desire with exuberance: to rush wildly into connection with others. Today, as I walk outside with my dogs, I still have a compulsion to connect with every person that I see: to wave, to say hello, to smile, to have a conversation. The toddler and little lost girl are with me today and they urge me to connect, to reach out into the expanse of the Universe and join in fellowship with my brothers and sisters, to be united and to be one.

And this is how Tribal Abundance was birthed, from my life experiences and the experiences I've had in the work world. My desire is to spark a passion in *you* to live with Tribal Abundance as well: to live, work, and connect in such a way that you are never alone.

For Reflection

What are some of the memories you have that have strongly influenced who you are today?

CHAPTER 2

The First Step Is Always the Hardest

"I've learned that people will forget what you said, people will forget what you did, but people will never forget how you made them feel."

—Maya Angelou

I pulled up to the restaurant and parked my car. I felt nervous and excited because today was the day I was speaking about my new program, Tribal Abundance. I had just twenty-five minutes to invite everyone into my experience. I took a deep breath, gathered all my materials, and walked into the restaurant, which doubled as a brewery.

The room was small, square and dark (even with the lights on), and filled with tables and chairs. There were six tables, with six to eight chairs at each, scattered throughout the room: perfect for the number of people I hoped would be attending. Each place was set with utensils and decorated with pink and orange; I could smell the hops and hear the buzzing sound of conversation in the restaurant.

Women began to arrive, filling the room with sounds of conversation and laughter. My heart lifted as each woman came in. I saw women that I knew, old friends, new acquaintances, women of all ages, shapes, sizes, and colors. Each woman was beautiful, each brought her own special gifts and uniqueness, and each one was there to connect, support, and collaborate. I was among my tribe.

Polka Dot Powerhouse (PDP) meetings had been going on in Albuquerque for almost a year. The organization had brought positive women together in my city, and called out to women who wanted to connect without having to deal with drama, scarcity mindsets, or competitiveness. It was a powerful, dynamic, engaging group. Because Tribal Abundance is about finding your tribe, working as a tribe, and having an abundance mindset rather than a scarcity mindset, that PDP meeting was the perfect place for me to share the Tribal Abundance mindset for the very first time.

Finding your tribe is a powerful thing; so many people feel disconnected from others, like they are outsiders, or like they just plain "don't belong." This was what drew me to PDP: it provides a place where positive, drama-free women can come together to support one another, to encourage one another, and to collaborate and connect. Like the Tribal Abundance concept, PDP is also about finding your tribe and connecting with like-minded people.

And that really is the heart of Tribal Abundance— connecting, supporting, collaborating and not competing. The tribal piece and the abundance piece are intertwined and inseparable. Being able to be a supportive and collaborative member of a tribe comes from having an abundance mindset, not one based upon the fear of scarcity.

An abundance mindset is the perspective that there *is enough* for everyone and there is no need to greedily grasp at things. It's about fostering an open heart and teaching your mind to trust that there *is no* lack. Living this mindset draws you to your tribe and draws your tribe to you. It attracts like-minded people to you… which is exactly how I found PDP.

And so, we went through the ritual of the meeting: making introductions, sharing connections and celebrations, talking about events and specials. And then it was my turn. I stood and began by asking everyone to close their eyes. As I walked around the room and began to tell a story, the soft sounds of the rainforest played through the small speaker I carried with me.

"Imagine that you are on the continent of Africa, in its very heart along the equator, in the Democratic Republic of Congo. And in that country, there is a rainforest, the Ituri Rainforest, which covers about twenty-four thousand square miles. That's about the size of West Virginia. The forest is a moist, humid region strewn with rivers and lakes.

"The forest has four layers. In the very top layer there are trees that are over 260 feet in height; that's about the height of the Hyatt Regency here in town. The next layer is dense and lush with trees reaching 145 feet. The next layer down is where lizards, birds, snakes, and some predators like the jaguar make their home. There are a lot of insects and the leaves of the trees in this layer are a lot bigger than those on the rainforest floor.

"And finally, you have the rainforest floor, the lowest level of the rainforest. It only gets 2% of the sun's light, but it's not dark, dim or gloomy. It glows with light. Kind of an otherworldly light.

"There are lots of animals in the rainforest: a forest giraffe, called okapi, many different species of antelopes, leopards, primates, including chimpanzees, a species of gorilla, and elephants. There are also 189 species of plants, including flowering plants, ferns, bamboo trees, and coconut trees. The forest is alive with presence.

"Now, I want you to stay in the rainforest, but go ahead and open your eyes. On that rainforest floor live a people called the BaMbuti (pronounced "BAA um booty"). They are pygmy hunter-gatherers, and they live in small tribes of fifteen to eighty. These forest people are nomadic, and at the beginning of the dry season they move deep into that lowest level of the forest to hunt.

"Once they arrive at their new camp, they focus and work together, putting up tents and getting settled. People choose where their huts will be, based on their familial relationships, and they gather the materials they need to build.

"They hunt together and everyone participates. They hunt in groups by setting nets between trees. Women and children drive antelope, forest giraffes, and other animals into the nets and the men use bows and arrows to kill the game they've captured.

"They trade this meat with farmers, for grains and vegetables. The forest people also gather and forage in the forest. Their favorite food is wild honey, and they are on a constant quest for it, and search for it according to the cycle of flowering trees.

"Everyone benefits from the hunt, no matter their role. In their small, tightly knit hunting band, survival can be achieved only by cooperation and by an elaborate system of reciprocal obligations which ensures that everyone has some share in the day's catch. Cooperation is the key.

"They trust that the forest will provide for them. 'When we are the Children of the Forest, what need have we to be afraid of it? We are only afraid of that which is outside the forest.' They are very familiar with their world and therefore they have no fear. 'The forest is a father and mother to us, and like a father or mother it gives us everything we need—food, clothing, shelter, warmth...and affection. Normally everything goes well, because the forest is good to its children, but when things go wrong there must be a reason.'

"When something negative happens, like illness strikes or game is scarce, the forest people believe it must be because the forest is sleeping and not looking after its children. What do they do? They wake it up.

And they wake it up by singing to the forest, and they do this because they want it to wake up happy. Then everything will be well and good again. They also sing to the forest when their world is going well because they want to share their happiness.

"They are connected to the forest in a spiritual way. All that is needed is to awaken it, and everything will come right. They have a simple approach when things go wrong. 'The forest is our home; when we leave the forest, or when the forest dies, we shall die. We are the people of the forest.'

"Children are parented by all adults. The very nature of a child's own nomadic hunting and gathering existence provides all the toughening up and education needed. A child's upbringing perfectly prepares him or her for the life they will lead.

"They put the good of *the whole* above the good of *the self.* They give thanks. Further, the BaMbuti regard fire as the most precious gift of the forest, and by offering it back to the forest they are acknowledging their debt and their dependence."

Next, I pointed out that we can incorporate these behaviors into our lives, even if our "forest" is the workplace and our lives might seem much more complex. Their behaviors are based on timeless principles that transcend technology and modern life. You can be a forest person in the midst of your modern, technologically advanced life.

As I spoke of the concepts of collaboration, support, and knowing one's purpose and place in the world, I could tell that these concepts were resonating with the women in the room. As I shared how those tribal behaviors could be lived out today and how they would enhance each person's life, I sensed a collective agreement, a deep resonation with these ancient principles. As I finished my talk, the music of the forest echoed in the hearts of the women in the room.

To conclude, I handed out a questionnaire I had created, which guides people to assess themselves and to identify their Tribal Abundance Quotient (see page 170 in Appendix A). This is a set of questions designed to give a baseline measure of "where you are now" and helps to identify areas in your life where you can make changes to increase your quotient. I asked the women to spend some time discussing their results in small groups at their tables. The buzz of conversation filled the room, and I heard laughter and sharing and could sense the opening of hearts and minds to concepts that were not new, yet were put forth in a unique way.

After sharing Tribal Abundance I felt completely

exhilarated. It felt as though my heart was bursting open, like a flower bursts open when it blooms. Seeing the joy in the others' eyes as Tribal Abundance resonated with them brought me metaphorically to my knees in gratitude. All along I had felt as though Tribal Abundance was divinely inspired and brought to life through my experiences of moving, being separated from loved ones, and searching for connection with others. A wave of joy flowed through me and reached the farthest corners of my heart, bringing me a sense of peace in the knowledge that I had accomplished my purpose. Spreading Tribal Abundance was clearly to become part of my future.

Bringing Tribal Abundance to PDP that day filled me with such incredible joy. Walking into that room, the love and support was palpable; I could sense it in an almost physical way. After the program, when people came up to me and thanked me, I felt as though I was living my life's purpose. Because yes, I want to share Tribal Abundance with the world so that people can work and play together with more love, compassion, and understanding. I have such a sense of joy and fulfillment when I facilitate a workshop and I can see in someone's eyes that they "get" it. They recognize that how we interact with others has to do with how we view the world and how we view ourselves.

I would love to see people in workplaces, all over the world, collaborating, being kind to one another, supporting, and encouraging one another. That is the type of workplace I envision, not one in which people feel disengaged, beaten down, marginalized, and disrespected. I love to see people live the best version of themselves, bringing their Best Selves to work and coming from a place of Tribal Abundance.

For Reflection

What are some "first steps" you've taken that have been a little scary for you? How did taking those steps make you feel?

CHAPTER 3

I Want to Play Bigger

"The first step towards getting somewhere is to decide that you are not going to stay where you are."

—*Chauncey Depew*

More than ten years earlier: "You've just lost me $10,000 worth of business!" my boss screamed at me.

I was stunned. I had simply taken a phone call in which someone cancelled their appointment. But because I had allowed that person to cancel without getting another appointment on the books, somehow, I had failed.

"There must be a better way," I thought to myself.

Five years later: I was working at yet another company.

"You need to get rid of her!" my boss yelled.

My heart sank. I couldn't believe I was hearing these words. My employee had made a minor, fixable mistake, but because egos were on the line she was being made a scapegoat. I was fighting for her and her job.

"There *must* be a better way," I thought again.

Thankfully I was able to make the case for saving my employee's job and I did not have to fire her. It was an experience that left a bitter taste in my mouth and while it had a positive outcome, it colored my experience of leadership.

And so it went. Over the years, I continued to come up against difficult situations in which people reverted to their worst selves and lashed out at others in fear.

The straw that broke the camel's back: I was working on a two-day training workshop with two of my male colleagues. The goal was to equip our employees with the tools and resources to enable them to succeed in their roles. As I headed home that night, I felt really good that we had successfully crafted the workshop in an instructionally sound manner and that I had stood firm on incorporating adult learning principles.

But, when I got to work the following morning, I found that my colleagues had changed the structure of the two days and revised the schedule, completely disregarding my input. I felt a warmth and a prickling feeling spread through my body and I began to tremble. I couldn't think straight; I was so angry I felt as though I didn't have any control over myself. Because the final structure had already been submitted and approved behind my back, I was unable to add in my input and they had their way.

"There must be a better way," I thought, yet again. This was the impetus I needed to go into business for myself. I had spent years gaining experience, pursuing and obtaining an advanced degree, and making many connections. It was now or never. I turned in my resignation just a few days later and never looked back. I was exhausted by the competitive need of others to be "right" and was disillusioned by the fear-based mindset that seemed to prevail. It was time for me to move on.

Initially, my business focus was on subcontracting. I had many connections and the work flowed to me. I did instructional design projects for one company and traveled all over the country. I did leadership development workshops and analysis projects for another company and traveled to California on a regular basis. I had small projects working for nonprofit organizations, and large projects working for big companies which required me to hire interns to help me. I was busy and working hard…and exhausted.

"There *must* be a better way," I thought as I fell into bed one night, spent.

At the time, I felt as though I wasn't making a lasting impact. Over and over I saw the same issues in organizations: people who were unhappy in their jobs and hated their bosses and coworkers; leaders who felt overwhelmed with the "people" stuff, helpless and ill-equipped to deal with conflict; disengaged employees, bullying others in the workplace; people who wouldn't "play" together nicely.

My heart's desire was to make a bigger impact and to change the workplace, one person at a time. My heart would break when someone would share their story with me, crying about how horrible things were and how unhappy they were with their work life. Those people found me and poured out their hearts. Whether it was because I was an outsider, a consultant, whether it was because I had a sympathetic ear and was good listener, or whether it was simply because I was there when people needed to unburden themselves, I heard similar stories over and over and over again.

"THERE MUST BE A BETTER WAY," I declared, and knew that my life's calling, my purpose, was being awakened by these stories of pain, confusion, hurt, and disillusionment. I was often drawn back to my Lucy Moment, a moment when all hope seemed like fragile old bones of the past. But now, I was a grown woman and I could do more than just sit in the pain; now, I could do something about it. I knew that I wanted to help shift things somehow, and to make a powerful impact in the world.

I knew I wanted to play bigger. I knew there was a better way.

A company that has leaders who operate from the scarcity model (fear that there is never enough) will eventually drive itself to extinction or madness because all of its resources will be depleted, just as someone desperate to be good enough physically can deplete herself of the very nutrients and energy needed to be physically fit. Someone desperate to be good enough for a mate depletes himself of the self-respect that would attract one. In the same way, a company desperate to "be enough" depletes itself of the very things that will make it successful.

The resource most depleted in this example is the group of employees who are overlooked inside the scarcity model. Neglected employees become needy, adapting their own scarcity models, thus forcing them to attempt success from a fear-based mindset that turns to self-interest and eventually wreaks havoc on their productivity and work relationships.

Perhaps you, too, work within a culture that is ever-striving to be better, always feeling the shortage, *the lack*—and thus you act out of your own scarcity model, forcing "success" from a depleted mindset, causing further depletion down the line. When I worked at one particular training company, by the end of the day I felt like a tube of toothpaste that had been squeezed completely dry. I had absolutely nothing left inside me and the only way I felt anything was by exercising my body into oblivion, pushing myself physically until I'd squeezed every last drop of energy out of my body. And then I would fall into bed exhausted, knowing I would wake up the following day to repeat the pattern all over again. I was becoming more and more depleted and I didn't know how to make it stop.

For example, it cost the Ik, as well. The Ik were once successful nomadic hunter-gatherers who made a living in the mountainous area of northern Uganda. Sadly, this tribe began to operate from the scarcity model when the winds of politics changed, and they were forced from their hunting grounds in 1962 when their land became part of a national park. They needed to change and adapt to their new circumstances, but they did *not* manage to do that.

Scared, and believing there was not enough for them to survive, these mountain people turned inward, becoming competitive and focusing on their individual needs, and eventually degenerating to the point where they would steal bread from the mouths of dying tribal members. Because there were two other tribes in the area that thrived, it is clear that it wasn't their circumstances that prevented them from flourishing. Rather, it was their belief in scarcity, that there wasn't enough, that caused them to focus on individual self-interest. The Ik barely survived as a tribe, and today are hanging on by a thread. Their scarcity mindset created a self-fulfilling prophecy of no longer being able to achieve abundance.

They were so unlike the BaMbuti tribe that I spoke about at the Polka Dot Powerhouse meeting. If you recall, the BaMbuti lived in the forest and thrived. These forest people did not live in fear because they trusted that the forest would provide for them—and they knew that they would take care of the forest. It never crossed their minds that they could not have enough, so generosity was possible. Everyone gave: everyone contributed to the good of the tribe and the forest, and as a result, everyone was taken care of. No one went hungry or experienced any kind of lack. It was more important to them to have peace among the tribe than for any one individual to be right or wrong, so when there were issues, they settled them together. In fact, no individual was singled out as either special or bad. The tribe, the whole, was exalted over the individual, and as a result, they cultivated consistent abundance.

Just like the Ik, companies become reactive, restrictive, and competitive when in scarcity mode. Employees focus on their own interests over the interests of the whole/tribe, leaving the landscape depleted and fractured. People are expected to fend for themselves, and those who don't can be seen as a burden and a hazard. ("You need to get rid of her!" to quote my former boss.) These were the experiences I had that led me to declare that there *must be a better way.*

And, just like the BaMbuti, there are companies that are collaborative and operate in an abundance model. Everyone gives, everyone contributes to the good of the organization, and everyone is taken care of. Imagine a workplace where this is the norm, where all employees operate in this way.

For Reflection

What are the experiences you've had that have motivated you to do things differently? To take steps in a different direction?

CHAPTER 4

Finding Your Tribe

"It's important to find your tribe."

—*RuPaul*

Inside the deep well in my grandparents' yard was where the milk was kept. The round grey slab of stone was about three feet high and there was a smaller stone covering the access hole in the center. Inside, there was a rope, and at the end of the rope was a bucket in which the bag of milk was kept. As I peered into the black hole of the well one day, my grandfather kept a firm grip on me. I saw nothing but darkness.

I could feel the coolness of the well wafting up and could hear the echo of a small stone as it dropped into the water far below. There was safety in the warmth of my grandfather's hand clasping mine, and I was not afraid to look down into the darkness as I was not alone. I felt courageous as I helped to pull the rope up and replace the heavy stone. My grandfather warned me to be careful and I thought that nothing bad could happen to me with my hand in his. *I am not alone.*

This experience with my grandfather, which I treasure to this day, happened at my grandparents' home in Hungary when I was nine years old. I felt like the luckiest girl in the world that I could travel with my family to visit my grandparents. It had been seven years since our last visit and this time my younger brother was also with us. Best of all, we were surrounded by cousins, aunts and uncles, and most importantly to me, our grandparents.

There are many times in our lives when we descend into darkness. As we peer down into the blackness there may not be the warm and loving grip of a grandfather to give us strength; we may be all alone. But we have to descend nonetheless, and we have to strengthen ourselves, hopefully developing courage over the years. If our courage fails us or we don't feel brave, we simply have to look around to see who can take our hand. I can remember the courage I took from my grandfather's firm grip; I knew he wouldn't let go unless I let go first. I walked through many life experiences imagining my hand firmly grasped in his.

An important element of Tribal Abundance is the concept of a family, a tribe. *Tribe.* What does that even *mean?* Wikipedia's definition is "a social division in a traditional society consisting of families or communities linked by social, economic, religious, or blood ties, with a common culture and dialect, typically having a recognized leader." Merriam-Webster online defines it as "a group of persons having a common character, occupation, or interest."

We used to live in small tribes of hunter-gatherers. We once relied on one another to survive and to thrive. We were successful when we collaborated with one another. Today, there are tribes who are linked by common interests like networking and social groups, tribes who are linked by religious ties, and tribes who are linked by family relationships, language, and culture. Many sacred religious texts emphasize the importance of not being alone: "And the Lord God said, 'It is not good that man should be alone.' "[1]

---

1   Scripture taken from the New King James Bible Version. Copyright © 1982 by Thomas Nelson.

When we are connected to our tribe, those moments of darkness and difficult times are easier to bear. We have someone to hold our hand—literally and figuratively—and all feels right with the world. We are at home.

For Reflection

What does the word "tribe" mean to you? How many different tribes do you feel part of?

CHAPTER 5

Finding Your Home

"He is happiest, be he king or peasant,
who finds peace in his home."

—*Johann Wolfgang von Goethe*

The concept of *home* was always a fuzzy one to me when I was younger. I knew that I lived in a home where my parents were and where my brothers and I played, and where we had lots of guests and social activity. I also knew that there was another home—Hungary, a whole other country—where my father's family and my cousins were. Hungary is connected to my heart. And yet, it wasn't a home where I spent a lot of time since I lived on the other side of the world. Even back when

I was in a crib, I began to have the inkling that *home* was more than just a physical location; it was where I felt connected and where I was not alone.

Growing up, I had a friend whose parents were divorced. It wasn't as common back then as it is now, and I remember being fascinated by the fact that she had two homes. In each home she had a bedroom that belonged to her; I never saw the bedroom she had in Arizona when she went to stay with her father, but she described it to me, stating that it didn't have any of her photos and mementos. She had to share her bedroom with her stepsister, which was a novelty for her as she was an only child. Eventually, she took mementos from her bedroom in New Mexico to her bedroom in Arizona to make it feel more like home. In a similar way, aside from Hungary, I had two homes: I was born in South Africa and spent the first ten years of my life there, and then we emigrated to the United States.

Have you ever watched a crumpled-up piece of paper being blown around by the wind? It blows quickly in one direction, pauses, and then is blown in another direction. Sometimes the gust of wind picks the paper up and it flies into the air, twirling around before settling in a spot on the ground. Then another gust drives it like a ball on a playing field, rolling it over and over in one direction, and then it shifts suddenly, moving the paper in a completely different direction.

I am that piece of paper. I've been blown across continents and oceans, have picked up and flown great distances, have moved in one direction in one country and then been blown in another direction to another country. I move along without restraint. I go where the wind sends me.

The wind picked me up in South Africa, the country of my birth, the country of many childhood memories. I can remember going to the library every week with my brothers. My mother drove us there, the three of us rolling around in the backseat in the days before passenger seat belts, child restraint systems, or car seats. A sharp braking of the car meant that we would all go flying, and we shrieked with laughter at the sensation. Then the real magic began as we entered the library and inhaled the unique scents of books and paper. Whole other worlds awaited us in those books.

I remember a trip to the Kruger Park with my family. My father let me sit on his lap and steer the car as he drove. I remember the feeling of excitement as I held the steering wheel and carefully made the twists and turns through the dirt roads. We saw elephants, giraffes, lions, rhinos, hippos, buck, buffalo, baboons, and monkeys.

We couldn't contain our excitement for each new sighting and we would scream with joy. Our hearts beat fast as we pressed our noses to the car windows and we fogged up the glass with our breath. Ever mindful of the rule to not roll down our windows, we felt protected by the glass (as we knew some of the animals viewed us as food) as the animals walked past us.

"You have such sharp eyes!" my parents told me as I pointed out the game I spotted. We stared into the trees, the long grass, and many plants as we sharpened our skills at spotting movement. We would look for the rustling of leaves, a shifting of the grasses that signaled a wild animal was near.

We heard the roar of lions, the thundering hooves of zebras, and through the open windows of our car (when we were allowed to open them), the rushing of the wind through the long grasses of the veldt. There were the sounds of drumbeats, singing, ululating, a chanting and rhythm that seeped into the very marrow of my bones and spread throughout my body. The sounds of Africa. This was my home. This was where I first began to see the right and the wrong of the world and to learn how it sometimes didn't align with my own inner compass of right and wrong. It's where I first learned that there are things in the world that can bring pain and things in the world that can bring joy. It was where I met Lucy.

In a split second the very meaning of the word "home" can change and all of a sudden, we are uprooted. South Africa is no longer my home, it is now the place where I am from and I have a new home. I have been transplanted and I can feel the trauma from my roots being ripped up and pulled away from the comfortable soil in which I lived. Plants can experience transplant shock when they are moved, and care has to be taken to disturb the roots as little as possible. There is a significant risk of a plant dying when it is transplanted and it is important to help it adjust to the shock so that it can flourish in its new home. Even though one may have a sense of excitement and anticipation about finding a new home, if their roots are damaged when they are "pulled up," there can be pain and loss.

For Reflection

What or where do you consider to be your home? What is it that makes it your home?

CHAPTER 6

Disorientation

"Change is always tough. Even for those who
see themselves as agents of change, the process
of starting a new thing can cause times of
disorientation, uncertainty and insecurity."

—*Joyce Meyer*

The wind also blew me to the US. Our plane touched
down in Albuquerque, New Mexico, and we were in
our new country.

Brown. Dusty. Hot.

When we stepped out of the airport I felt a wave
of heat hit me—it almost knocked me over with its
intensity. It was hard to breathe.

Everything was brown. I came from a city where the streets were lined with trees, creating an arch of green through which to walk and drive. In the springtime, the jacaranda trees were lush with their huge purple blossoms creating a magical scene of purple-lined streets. As the flowers fell they created a purple carpet, enveloping the streets and softening the city landscape. The earth was rich and dark brown, filled with the goodness that plants thrived on and everywhere you turned there was green.

Back "home" my brothers and I had run around barefoot in our front and back yards, our feet cushioned by luxuriant grass. The garden was filled with bright beautiful colors. On Sunday after church we would drive to Zoo Lake and feed the ducks. The lake was surrounded by grass and an abundant forest of weeping willows and many other types of trees.

I came from a country with beautiful coastlines: the drive from Johannesburg to Durban was an adventure. We would pass the Drakensberg mountains in the distance as we wound our way down through the curves of Van Reenen's Pass. We would stop at the Valley of a Thousand Hills and gaze over the rolling hills that seemed to go on forever into the mist in the distance. As we'd near the coast, the vegetation impossibly became even lusher and greener. We would keep our eyes peeled because each one of us wanted to be the first one to spot a monkey in the trees that lined the streets. But now—

Hot. Brown. Strange.

The high desert landscape of New Mexico was foreign to me. It had sharp edges—cacti, thorny bushes, and something called "goat head stickers" that could easily pierce sensitive skin—and dry, pale, dusty ground. I had never felt heat like it before and the dry air and high altitude seized my lungs and made it hard for me to breathe.

My father's new boss picked us up at the airport in Albuquerque and drove us the seventy-five miles south to Socorro, the small town that was to become our new home. Before arriving at the house we were to rent for the next three years, he drove us around the town. Small-town Socorro in 1977 was a far cry from Johannesburg, South Africa and years later my parents told us that their first thoughts of that little tour were, "My God, have we made the biggest mistake of our lives?"

One year we had stopped in the Drakensburg mountains in South Africa on our drive to Durban and for the first time in my life I saw snow. We were in summer clothes and were shivering while squealing with joy as we touched and tasted the few flakes that had somehow managed to fall...

…And one morning in New Mexico, several months after we had arrived, we opened our windows to a beautiful world of white. The snow had fallen overnight and covered the earth in a beautiful, white, glistening and sparkling blanket. We quickly bundled up and ran outside; there was a quiet stillness and the world seemed an enchanted and mystical place.

We joined the neighborhood children on the slopes of the golf course near our home and exhausted ourselves rolling down the hills, throwing snowballs, and building snowmen. We returned home hours later, shivering and cold, yet exhilarated by the magic of winter.

This new home was not so bad after all.

There is a transition that happens when we move. Whether it's moving to a new country, a new home or school, a new company, or even to a different department at work, there's a shift that has to be made. There's a period of disorientation when things feel new and different. A plant that has been transplanted must be nurtured and encouraged to grow, its root system nourished so that it can establish itself and thrive. Like with plants, with each move you make there is a small part of you that is ripped away, that is left behind, and you can always sense that missing piece. Yet, as you are transplanted, your roots begin to reach down and reestablish you, planting you firmly so that you may absorb the nutrients that you need to flourish. Your home is where you are connected, where you are not alone.

Tribal Abundance helps with this process of transplantation by providing a light at the end of the tunnel, a vision of what is possible during the time of adjustment and transition. When the core principles and values that are the framework for your life are about connecting and living in abundance, your "root system" will be strong. While you might sway with strong winds, you will not be painfully uprooted.

For Reflection

What are the ways in which you've been transplanted? How did you deal with it and how long did it take you to feel comfortable again?

CHAPTER 7

A New Normal

"I think you always have to be innovating
and adapting and improving. You can't stay
the same."

—*George Allen*

Starting over again would mean adjusting to a new culture and country. Starting over again was to become my new normal.

"Scoot over."

I was startled. A nine-or ten-year-old, someone standing behind me in the queue (which I later learned was a "line") spoke those words to me and I had no idea what they meant.

"I beg your pardon?" I responded, the way I had been taught to, as it had been drilled into my head that *this* was the polite way to respond.

"Scoot over!"

I still didn't know what he meant and a sense of fear and panic rose up in me.

Having recently emigrated from Johannesburg, South Africa to tiny Socorro, New Mexico, everything was new. Even the clothes and shoes. (Whoppers. I remember the name of the shoes I wore because I recall the excitement my brothers and I had when we eventually went shopping with my mother and bought the Whoppers shoes that *everyone* was wearing.) Everything I wore was different from what everyone else was wearing. Wrong somehow. Even my accent set me apart as different and I hated that. I wanted to fit in. And there I was, hearing words that I didn't know the meaning of. It was as though I was listening to a foreign language, but I could understand bits and pieces here and there, and my brain had to work overtime to fit the pieces together to understand it all. What was happening to me? I couldn't understand why things were so difficult for me. I had left my school, McAuley House, as the top student in my class. I was smart. So why was this all so difficult?

What I came to understand years later is that I really *was* learning a foreign language via the immersion process. I had to pick up a whole new vocabulary, learn a different way to pronounce the words I already knew so that others would understand me, and I had to be able to quickly figure out what others were saying by reading nonverbal cues since I didn't always understand the words they used.

Yet somehow, we were both speaking English—that young boy asking me to "scoot over" and me responding, "I beg your pardon?"—that crazy language that is an amalgamation of many other languages, a language that has evolved over the years and has swallowed up words and expressions from all over the globe to become a hodgepodge mix of grammar rules and syntax and exceptions to the rules.

I remember while living and teaching in Hungary (many, many years later) I tried to teach my English students some of the intricacies of English grammar. When they shook their heads in confusion because it didn't make sense, I would respond, "I know it doesn't make sense, it just is!"

And it just is. Words have many meanings and pronunciations that mark where you are from or where you live. It's a living, breathing, dynamic thing, this crazy, beautiful language we speak called English. It baffles and frustrates those who try to grasp its secrets and learn its twists and turns. Yet it's not something that can be conquered without a fierce battle and a continued watchfulness as it changes shape and form and easily escapes from one's grasp. It's only when you reach a certain comfort level that the language is truly yours. It's like trying on a new piece of clothing that doesn't fit very well—it's a little too tight in places and too loose in others—and that doesn't flatter. You try to button it up and it stretches and pulls and gapes and you give up and consider discarding it because it's too hard to try to make it work.

But if you persist and pull it a little this way and that, perhaps loosen or take in a seam, and work to make it fit…one day you'll realize that you've been wearing that piece of clothing and suddenly it is so comfortable and fits so well. It has become a part of your wardrobe and moves with you as you move, seamlessly becoming part of your identity. This process of becoming comfortable after making some adjustments is how change becomes a part of who you are and your identity.

The journey of moving and transition is not an easy one and being transplanted is difficult. Yet with each move, each time you are transplanted, you learn and grow and begin to see patterns. I used to joke that I was a human chameleon. I would adapt and change to my environment, taking on the "colors" of each new home I called my own. Those colors were language, customs, and habits. Yet even though I changed colors outwardly as the chameleon does, I was still the same person inside. A chameleon doesn't change what it is, it just adapts to its surroundings and blends in.

There's a part of your ego that has to die with these experiences. The ego jumps up and shouts, "Look at me! Look at me!" Yet as the outward color changes, the goal is to blend in and adapt. This process is antithetical to having the spotlight on you; if you were to put a spotlight on a chameleon that has blended in, would you see it? The goal is to adapt so completely that you don't stand out.

This concept is a key element of what I bring to my work. As a person who facilitates groups, my goal is to help them understand one another, connect better, and communicate more clearly. I was molded by the human-chameleon coping mechanism and bring some of that concept to the groups I facilitate. For example, I use an exercise in groups where individuals are paired up with someone who has similar results on their assessment report. They discuss the traits that they see has having the most positive impact on their workplace behavior, and also the traits that might detract from their best workplace behavior. The sound of their discussions usually becomes loud and engaged, and there is often lots of laughter and enjoyment. When that discussion is done, I then pair people up with someone whose results on their assessment report are very different and they have the same discussion. What is always enlightening is how the pairs can always find similarities even though "on paper" they are so different.

I remember one situation specifically where there were two people paired up who appeared very reluctant to participate in this activity with one another. My intuition told me that they just did not like one another and avoided interacting. Yet as I circulated around the room to listen to all the discussions, I noticed that this pair was having an engaging conversation. At the end of the discussion time I asked, as I always do, if anyone had an insight, new learning or observation to share. I wasn't surprised when the pair spoke up and talked about how they did not think they had anything in common, yet had discovered that they were more alike than they originally thought.

While I would never tell someone to change who they are, this exercise illustrates that we are often more similar than we think. And so rather than looking for how we are different, I encourage people to become chameleons as they adapt and look for the ways in which they are similar and can blend in. I challenge them to learn the language, customs, and habits, to become enculturated. And then if you identify ways in which the culture needs to change, you come from a platform of having experienced and lived in that workplace culture. Others may take a different approach; I know what has worked well for me is the human-chameleon coping mechanism.

For Reflection

In what ways have you had to adapt to new circumstances or situations? How did you cope with the change?

CHAPTER 8

Language Connects Us to Our Tribe

"The development of language is part of the development of the personality, for words are the natural means of expressing thoughts and establishing understanding between people."

—Maria Montessori

I can hear so many sounds. *Clicks...*

It's like listening to a babbling stream, the sound of the wind blowing over the dry sands of the Kalahari Desert, or the sound of waves, crashing on the shores in Umhlanga Rocks. I am mesmerized by the sounds.

Sotho, Zulu, Xhosa, Ndebele, Sotho, Tsona, Tswana, Afrikaans, English, these are the sounds I hear.

"Look there's a witch doctor!" A witch doctor? A thrill rises in me as I gaze at an old black man, his shoulders covered with the pelt of a leopard, his head crowned with an elaborate headdress. He carries a stick.

The witch doctor is the one who gives our maid "good muti" to cure her illness. He is the wise man.

These are the sounds of my childhood, these are the sounds of my country.

***

I heard the music and rhythm of different languages around me while growing up in South Africa. Even today I am thrilled when I hear someone speaking a language I don't understand. I remember hearing the bible story of the Tower of Babel when I was a little girl. My brothers and I slowly turned the pages of our illustrated children's bible to read the story, and the colorful image of people building a tower that would reach to the heavens, that would reach God, is burned into my mind. I never understood why God didn't want people to reach him, but I was glad that different languages were created because of it. And when I hear the rhythm of a language I don't understand I am taken back to my youth and the cacophony of sounds that were part of my world.

Just as the sounds of different languages resonated for me and made me feel I was home, our language and how we communicate is an important part of creating and building our tribe at work.

Have you ever had an experience where you've felt completely misunderstood? Perhaps you tried and tried to communicate something and you just couldn't succeed. It's frustrating and there's often a desire to just give up, or maybe you try to keep talking, saying the same things over and over, hoping desperately that they'll eventually understand you.

I remember working with a client who was frustrated by the fact that her team, and one team member in particular, didn't seem to understand her and often misconstrued her words. She laughingly said it was as though she was speaking a foreign language to them. And although she laughed as she said it, I could feel her aggravation and disappointment that she was not able to get her team to understand her. I challenged her to take a different approach the next time she communicated with her team, and especially with that one team member, making one small shift in how she approached the conversation. "Take a coaching approach," I suggested. "Rather than just trying to get the information across and 'telling them something,' instead, ask them questions and paraphrase what you've heard them say to check for understanding." She agreed to try this strategy and promised to report back during our next session.

When she reported back, it was not only as though a lightbulb had gone off, it was as though she had moved from complete darkness into the brightest light. Her whole approach to communication had completely shifted and she was happy to share that she had had many successful conversations since we last met.

Developing a language, a way to communicate, is a crucial piece in building a tribe. I find it intriguing that the core issue in many dysfunctional teams is the lack of clear and honest communication. Communication seems to be the topic that most people want to learn more about, and it's often mentioned by clients as the area in which they want to grow. When we are young we aren't really taught about communication in school, other than perhaps saying "Please" and "Thank you" and learning other well-worn phrases. If we are raised in a home where our parents are good communicators and can model that for us, we definitely have a leg up on building our communication skills. But what I've noticed is that most people struggle in this area and it's no surprise when our role models may not have been good communicators, our teachers and friends may not be good communicators, and even the language that we hear on television and in movies is not always a good model for us to follow.

I've always been fascinated by language and the words people use when they communicate; perhaps it comes from growing up in a home with a parent for whom English was not their first language, and maybe it's because I grew up bilingually (at least until school age when English began to dominate). Either way, listening to words and languages and their sounds always send a thrill through me. And once I recognized that I was not always a good communicator it became a quest for me to learn how to grow in this area. It's a continuing quest as we are not "done" at some point; there isn't a pinnacle to reach or a race to finish, it's a learning journey that we are on for the rest of our lives.

Because communication is such an essential part of working and living with others, we will come back to it and examine it in depth in upcoming chapters. For now, I want to leave you with the idea that there is great beauty to be had in all aspects of communication.

For Reflection

How is your personality expressed through the language you use? In what ways do you feel you could be a better communicator?

CHAPTER 9

Going Home

"Going home and spending time with your family and your real friends keeps you grounded."

—Jennifer Ellison

Over the years there was a yearning in me, a constant urge to go back to where it had all begun in South Africa. But, it was eleven years before I was able to return. My parents and younger brother had spent a six-month sabbatical in SA in 1986 and although I had desperately wanted to go with them, they told me that my college education was more important. I was in my first year of university and it was important to them that I stay focused. While I understood this on an intellectual level, my heart longed for Africa, for the sights, sounds, and smells of my home. Since we'd moved, I felt like a misfit, an outsider in some ways, and it felt as though going back to SA was something I needed to do. I was still learning to be the human-chameleon.

So, it was no surprise to my family when I declared that I would be moving to SA for a year once I completed my university studies and got my undergraduate degree. I wasn't drawn to find a job in the US, and although I was ambitious about beginning my career, it was more important to me to reconnect with my country of birth.

I had no idea that the year I was to spend in South Africa would be one of momentous change and transition around the world: State President F.W. de Klerk, who had come to office only a few months earlier, announced the goal of the end of apartheid. On February 11, 1990, Nelson Mandela was released from prison. The end of communist rule in Hungary had happened on October 23, 1989 when the Republic of Hungary was proclaimed. The fall of the Berlin Wall occurred on November 9, 1989, and the world was filled with hope. As I watched on television while Nelson Mandela walked free, the tears rolled down my cheeks and I felt as though I would burst with joy.

I spent a short time in Hungary on my way back to the US from Africa, and the change I felt was palpable. There was a buzz, an energy in the air, a sense of excitement as the possibilities for a new political future took shape. My cousin Laci was involved with the Young Democrats party and his passion and excitement were contagious.

It made me realize that governments could change, that people could affect positive change and bring about a better world. Without being able to clearly articulate it at the time, I recognized that the passion and energy of the world changers beat in my heart as well. I too had a vision for a better world and the essence of this remained with me and became the foundation for Tribal Abundance. Rather than accepting the status quo and being miserable in a job (or a country) that isn't fulfilling us, we can stand up and make a change.

There was a burning inside me, a desire to want to make a positive difference in the world. It felt as though there was more to this life than just having a career, getting married, having children. I felt a strong tug on my heart to make an impact, to positively influence others. As it was the days before the Internet, I pored over pamphlets and brochures and mailings, trying to find an organization through which I could make a difference.

I thought about joining the Peace Corps but found out that as I was not yet a US citizen, I was not eligible. I looked into the UN Volunteers but the amount of paperwork involved felt overwhelming. Because it wasn't a passion, a dream, I didn't have the drive to jump through all the hoops.

It was while I was in South Africa—my post-college gap year—that I felt the call to full-time ministry. I saw the world changing all around me, was especially impacted by the fall of the Berlin Wall and Nelson Mandela's release, and I had a hope for the future of the world. I wanted to be an active participant in the change. As I watched the television coverage of people knocking away chunks of the wall and flooding through the checkpoints I could feel a stirring in my heart. The wall was a physical metaphor for separation and as I watched the wall coming down and people coming together, I was inspired to be part of the movement of the end of communist rule. These were ordinary people like me, taking a stand against an oppressive system. And I felt the call to go "home" again, and this time the home that was calling me was Hungary.

For Reflection

What is most important to you about where you call home? Are you inspired to be better/do more or make a change when you go home?

CHAPTER 10

Having a Calling

"Whatever your calling is as a service,
follow it—that's beautiful."

—*Hill Harper*

It was soon after Nelson Mandela was released that I visited my cousin in Cape Town. I took an overnight bus, and while waiting for the bus to depart I noticed that there was a large group of people gathering. All of a sudden, they began to *toyi-toyi* (a dance step characterized by high-stepping movements, typically performed at protest gatherings or marches) and move down the street. I was swept up in the energy and excitement and began to move along with the crowd. There was a sense of freedom that called to me, and I wanted to stand in solidarity with my brothers and sisters. We toyi-toyied down the street, and the sounds of ululating and singing swirled around me, enveloping me in the sounds of South Africa. As I looked around, I saw joy on the faces of the hundreds, if not thousands, of people around me, their faces—from the darkest ebony to the lightest mocha, with a few white faces sprinkled in between—shining brightly in the sun.

And that image remained with me when I returned to live in the United States. I still had a desire to make a positive difference in the world and what that meant for me back then was going into full-time ministry. I chose to put a career on hold because it didn't feel as though I would be able to make the kind of impact I wanted to make while climbing the corporate ladder. I felt a much stronger pull to the world of full-time ministry and began to reach out and request information on how I could make that dream come true.

A small organization, International Teams, somehow came to my attention amidst the avalanche of mailings I was receiving from different mission organizations. I was back in New Mexico and had gotten an entry-level position at a training company. It would have been a great place for me to grow my career, yet I knew that I was there for a short time only. I was committed to my path and my focus was on raising the funds and support to make that happen. I spoke with one of the International Teams' advisors, Jeannie, and got excited about the possibility of moving to Hungary with a team. Even back then the thought of doing something with others was much more appealing to me than going it alone. The seed that had been planted when I was a toddler in my crib, of wanting to be with others, had grown and flourished, influencing the decisions I made and the paths that I chose. I was becoming a person who weighed the factors of relationship and connection into making any decision and I was drawn to the idea of working on a team of people who all had the same goals and desires.

Although I have always been fiercely independent, I've still never wanted to be alone. While traveling all over the world, often by myself, there has still been a desire to reach out to others. This has led to fascinating conversations with many people of all walks of life. Whether it was someone I sat next to in church or on a plane, or someone I bumped into in the grocery store or at an event or party, I would be drawn to finding out their stories. How did we both end up in the same place at the same time? What were our journeys like, how were they alike, and how were they different?

As an adult I understand that it's my extroversion that drives this need to connect. And while that need may look very different for an introvert, as humans we are social creatures and cannot live in isolation. In fact, think about the punishment of solitary confinement for those who are incarcerated. There have been many research studies conducted on the effects of extreme isolation, and they find that it's not uncommon for individuals to hallucinate, have panic attacks, and have difficulties with thinking, concentration and memory. Those in solitary confinement engage in self-mutilation at much higher rates than other prisoners and account for nearly half of prison suicides. The bottom line: isolation is not good for the human psyche!

I filled out all the paperwork and submitted my application. I can remember the incredible joy I felt when I received the call that I had been accepted into the program and that I would be moving to Prospect Heights, Illinois, to undergo their four-month training program. It felt as though everything in my life was lining up the way I wanted it to, and that my hopes and desires were being fulfilled.

I spent the next five years in Budapest, Hungary, working with a team whose focus was on establishing an evangelical Christian church. I also taught English and led small bible study groups. Those years were some of the best of my life as I was surrounded by like-minded people who wanted to make a difference in the world. I had certainly found my tribe and was accomplishing fulfilling work that was in alignment with my desire to serve.

It can be a challenge to find one's path and to get to a place where we feel as though we are fulfilled and making a difference in the world. And I don't believe that there's a "formula" that someone can follow to accomplish this. It's often in the twists and turns, the roadblocks, obstacles, and failures that we discover our path. And while we may have a very specific destination in mind as we begin the journey, it's not unusual to find that destination changing. Like every journey we embark upon, we can be fully prepared and yet still have things go awry. When it comes to finding your path, I believe the only "rule" is to keep going. Keep taking steps towards your destination even when you've lost your way, even when you're not sure where you're going, and even when you're tired and don't feel as though you can continue. Keep going. You don't have to take big steps, and you may need to stop and reflect, but don't give up.

For Reflection

Do you feel as though you have a calling? If so, when did you first discover it? Were there roadblocks you had to overcome in order to do your calling?

CHAPTER 11

Where Do You Belong?

"Language, identity, place, home: these are all of a piece—just different elements of belonging and not-belonging."

—*Jhumpa Lahiri*

I don't remember the first time I heard the word "refugee" but I know that it was connected to my father. There was something magical and special about that word although I didn't completely understand what it meant. I just knew that it set my father apart and made him different from everyone else's father. I felt so lucky that my father was a refugee; it made him, and by default me, special. Merriam-Webster defines a refugee as "one that flees; especially, a person who flees to a foreign country or power to escape danger or persecution."

During the Hungarian Revolution of 1956, the youth fled the country. They did not want to live under an oppressive political system and escaped via Austria in droves. My father tells the story of how, when he was twenty-four years old, he escaped his country with two friends and two suits (which he wore, one on top of the other); they snuck past a guard tower in the dead of night and considered it a miracle that they were not caught. I can clearly picture the tall guard tower that they snuck past to enter into a country of freedom: Austria.

Other than those two suits, he left Hungary with nothing. I can't believe the amount of faith and courage it must have taken to walk away from everything—family, friends, an almost-completed Master's degree—and to begin again. When I look at photos from that time I can see young people with hope, fear, and expectation in their eyes. I see images of a beautiful city ravaged by conflict, of Russian tanks and freedom fighters; I can see the hope crushed by the powerful Soviet machine.

Thousands of freedom fighters stood together and resisted the Russian tanks that rolled into the city of Budapest to quash the rebellion, and while their struggle and battle was ultimately crushed—over 2,500 Hungarians were killed and over 200,000 fled as refugees—what they accomplished in the twelve days they drew together was powerful, perhaps one of the defining events of the Cold War. The people of Budapest nearly succeeded against the Soviet empire, and clearly demonstrated to the world the failure of Communism.

It can often feel as though we are fighting a revolution in our day-to-day lives, having to gird ourselves as if for battle to face the day; feeling as though we are being crushed by tanks through the brutal encounters we face. We must find a way to stay strong in the face of the struggle.

Most young children don't know what the word "refugee" means, but it was a word that is woven into every one of my childhood memories. I knew it meant leaving your country and leaving your family in the dark of night. It wasn't until many years later that I grasped the significance of the revolution of 1956 and what it meant to the country of Hungary and to the political scene of the world. It was always very personal, a part of me, a part of my family, and a part of who I was.

I know I've felt that I need to flee sometimes, to leave behind the danger or persecution I experience and find someplace safer. I know you've probably felt like that, too. The desire to flee can be so strong that you feel it in every cell of your body; your body is on high alert and adrenaline is coursing through your veins, you feel your heart rate increase and you can sense anxiety, maybe even panic, in the pit of your stomach.

It's especially disheartening to hear that people feel this way about the places they work, that they don't feel safe or protected. They don't feel that their workplace is a place of refuge and instead they want to flee.

I find it ironic that the words "refuge" and "refugee" are so similar, yet their meanings are worlds apart. One small letter added to the end of refuge and the word becomes something entirely different. And how like our own lives—where one small thing added in can give it an entirely different meaning?

I've always loved the word serendipity: it rolls off the tongue so beautifully and its definition is powerful. It's the phenomenon of making desirable discoveries by accident: good fortune, luck. It's those small serendipitous things that occur that can give our lives an entirely different meaning. Serendipity happens between that one letter change—the extra e in refugee versus refuge—and in those day-to-day moments in our lives when we least expect it. It's the golden thread weaving through our life, connecting it all together.

So for all those who want to flee, and those who have fled and are refugees from your places of work, I invite you to search for refuge, to find that place where you have shelter and protection.

The first step is always reaching down deep into yourself, identifying what's wrong. And like the young Hungarians in 1956 who recognized something was wrong with their political system and then joined others who felt the same way, you can find your tribe of fellow refugees, people who are fleeing the workplaces where they're not appreciated, ignored, not respected, minimized, not supported, not encouraged. Identify what's wrong and then find the power in your tribe, the collective, the people who are going through similar experiences and feel lost and alone just like you do. There is strength in numbers and the support from your tribe helps you feel less alone. Just like the BaMbuti who worked together, supported one another, and collaborated, when you find your tribe, you are no longer alone.

A friend of mine once privately shared some stories with me about the struggles she was having at work. She broke down and cried as she talked about the different experiences that had made her feel as though she was not valued or appreciated. She had been pouring herself into her career and was working hard to make a difference in the workplace, and yet she desperately wanted to flee her position and find somewhere else where she could flourish. Although this was before Tribal Abundance, I still remember that as I listened and then offered advice, the principles were all there: find your tribe, connect with others like you, believe that there is something better out there. And as she embarked on her job-change journey I continued to encourage her. I was delighted when she found a new position where she felt appreciated and valued. She had found her tribe at work.

For Reflection

What do you feel is important about belonging?

CHAPTER 12

Finding Connection

"People tend to work in teams, in a collaborative way, in an informal network. If you create an environment like that, it's much more effective and much more efficient."

—*Jim Mitchell*

"That bloody foreigner!" My father heard these words working in the mines in Northern England. He describes feeling awkward and then realizing with relief that it was meant for those from southern England who were the "foreigners." The label "foreigner" seems to stick to a person who speaks English with an accent;

not everyone can be open and accept someone who doesn't sound like them. I see it every day, and I've lived it vicariously through my father's journey. Is this the reason that I long to fit in and belong? Perhaps. But I still carry that word "refugee" around like a talisman, knowing that it's part of my father's story.

How often do you feel disconnected at work? You're working hard and doing your best, but somehow you don't fit in. Just as it was a challenge for my father—and for me—to fit into our adopted cultures, it can be a challenge to fit into a work culture.

"I hate my boss!" one client said, and I could see the exhaustion and pain in her eyes. My heart sank as I heard yet another story of how miserable someone was at work. There's part of me that wants to jump in and fix things and offer the "three easy steps to get along with your boss" approach, yet there's also that part of me that acknowledges it's not so easy, and sometimes people just want to be listened to, to be heard.

And once I've listened to the stories and felt the pain and loneliness and frustration—sometimes even desperation—of the walking wounded, I stop and reflect and imagine a workplace where people can thrive, where people are connected and support one another, where people can excel in their work and be high performers, or just do the best job they're capable of doing, and in that way, make a contribution.

It's about living as a tribe.

Recently one my clients said, "He doesn't understand what it means to function in a team," about one of his employees. We were discussing some workshops that he wanted to hold for his employees and we were deciding on what it was that his team needed. When I design a workshop the key questions are always, "What's the end goal? What do you want employees to get out of this? What behavior do you want to see them display as a result?"

The answers to these questions help me to get to the root of what is going on with their team. It helps me to determine how tribal the team is (or not) and how to implement the Tribal Abundance program. It's part of the Taking Stock and Building a Tribe step in the process, which I'll cover in more detail in Chapter 23.

It was a comment on the employee's "unwillingness to function as a collaborative team member" and instead "he wanted only to focus on his own individual success" that got me thinking more about tribal behavior. I'll share more about building a tribal culture in other chapters; this was just one of those aha moments when I realized that so many work teams *don't* operate as a tribe.

Often there is competition and a desire for individual success that causes their leaders to pull their hair out in frustration. Yet, I think this non-tribal behavior is often the norm and what most people seem to expect. Creating a tribal culture involves getting buy-in from the members of your team because they may come from the perspective that a tribe is *not* a good thing. One of the first things we do in my Tribal Abundance Experience workshop is talk about a tribal culture versus an individualistic culture and about how research supports the success of a tribal culture in the workplace, as well as in our personal lives. Not everyone may agree that a tribal culture is best, yet if all team members are willing to commit to it for their team's sake it makes a huge impact on the evolution of the team.

I took a course recently called *Conversational Intelligence*®. It was based on the book of the same name by Dr. Judith Glaser. While there were many interesting things to learn, one concept that really struck me is how our heartbeats align and sync up with someone we are connected to. When you are happy, the brain releases oxytocin—the feel-good hormone—and you are washed in a chemical bath of wonderful feeling.

"There is new research that says that the more we elevate oxytocin or the more we give support to someone who is having difficulty or challenges, that our own bodies will go up to a higher state— there's such a natural desire in humans to feel good with others and be with others. We can, without asking someone to stop doing something, bring them up to a conversation that has a higher resonance with the oxytocin—and people want to be there!"

— Judith Glaser

You've felt it before, perhaps without even knowing what was happening. You were in conversation with someone and you felt so incredibly in synch with them. Unconsciously you began to mirror them: to stand like they were standing and to use the same gestures. You were incredibly connected to them.

You were connected to your tribe.

For Reflection

What does working on a team, being part of a tribe, mean to you?

CHAPTER 13

Finding Your Place

"Roots are not in landscape or a country, or a people, they are inside you."

—*Isabel Allende*

When I was in high school I got a part-time job at the local Kentucky Fried Chicken in Socorro, New Mexico. It was a chance for me to make some money of my own and to have a little financial freedom. Babysitting gigs were few and far between and I had very specific goals: I wanted a car and I wanted to go to Hungary. I had a yearning for something more and the tiny town of Socorro, New Mexico, was not big enough for me to fulfill my dreams and aspirations. There was a whole world out there—including Hungary and South Africa, that I had left behind—and I needed to spread my wings and fly.

With each paycheck I received I watched my savings account grow. I loved the independence working gave me—something that has stayed with me my whole life—and I was thrilled as that account balance increased and gave me more options. I worked at KFC for almost three years, most of my high school years. Learning how to juggle homework and a part-time job was difficult, and I was grateful that homework and studying came easily to me. On weekends when my friends were out having fun and I had just gotten off a shift and was exhausted, well, then I didn't feel so great. But the fun I had with my coworkers and the freedom I experienced financially more than made up for the struggles. And that bank balance continued to grow until I was able to purchase an airline ticket for a one-month-long trip to Hungary the summer before my senior year in 1984.

As the plane touched down in Budapest, tears welled and my throat felt tight. I was so excited yet also anxious and unsure. It was still the height of the Cold War, and I was traveling to Communist Hungary. I was like a tree left to grow freely and unrestrained; I was not used to the "rules" of a country where you could not be free.

As I walked out of baggage claim I was greeted by a sea of relatives—familiar and loved faces—and each one grabbed me and kissed both my checks. In a daze, I was handed down the line to greet everyone.

Later, I sat in the backseat of a car with my cousin Tündi and she excitedly pulled out a set of mini Hungarian-English dictionaries. She was prepared for us to communicate! Tündi's olive skin had already been darkened by the summer sun and her bright blue eyes sparkled as she handed me the English-to-Hungarian volume so that I could look up any words that weren't familiar to me. Her chocolate brown hair was loose and long, halfway down her back, and it created a curtain around her as she leaned forward to find the words she didn't know in English. I couldn't believe this beautiful creature was related to me and during that summer she became more than just my cousin, she became an older sister.

Memories of the month in Hungary are numerous. Every moment was precious to me…especially those spent in my grandparents' home in Balassagyarmat, where I visited all my cousins, and laughed with my grandfather as he told me my cousin Zoli was "mafla" (which means "gullible"). We went to Lake Balaton where everyone spent their summers, and I bounced from one family's home to the next, enjoying time with my cousins splashing around in the lake, riding bicycles, playing badminton, eating ice-cream and lángos—a delicious fried dough smothered with sour cream and cheese—and speaking lots and lots of Hungarian.

With no other English speakers around—and my cousin's Hungarian-to-English dictionary collecting dust—my six-year-old level of Hungarian rapidly developed into a fluent, although not perfect, expression of my "father tongue." It was 1984 and Hungary was still under communist rule; behind the Iron Curtain, it was almost untouched by many things in the western world. I was surprised by the lack of certain things—soft toilet paper, bananas, oranges, any fruit that wasn't locally grown—and delighted by what I found there that I couldn't get at home in the United States: turo rudi, a cottage cheese-filled chocolate bar, banana-flavored toothpaste, and a television show called "Esti Mese" (Bedtime Story) made for kids that included a cute cartoon teddy bear that brushed its teeth and gargled before it settled down to watch a story that we then all watched together.

I remember a conversation I had with my aunt and uncle—Tündi's parents—about my job at KFC. In Hungarian culture, money is not a taboo subject and people ask questions about how much you make and how much you pay for certain things. When I answered their question about how much I made at KFC and they translated the dollar amount to Hungarian forints, they exclaimed that my monthly earnings at my part-time job was more than their two monthly salaries combined. It was moments like that one that opened up my eyes to the great big world out there and gave me a more global perspective.

As I left my grandparents' home to travel back to the US, my grandparents walked outside with me into the street. There were tears in my grandfather's eyes as he said, "I don't think we're ever going to see you again." A pain swept through me and I couldn't hold back the tears. I realized he was right. This visit had been a gift— a peek into the lives of my family who were separated from me. The hollowness I had experienced from being separated from my grandparents had been temporarily filled. It was extremely difficult to leave them again.

From a very young age I knew that those I love often did not live near to me. First, I left my friends and family behind in South Africa, then I was separated from my family in Hungary.

It's funny how in today's world, distance is so much less of a factor. With Skype, my father could have been connected to his brother in Hungary on a daily basis. With the magic of e-mail and messaging apps I can now reach out to the other side of the globe and connect with my cousins.

Connection: a desire to be close and have relationships. It's been a deep and perpetual desire for me, a yearning to be part of a tribe. Having the opportunity to visit my family in Hungary when I was young helped me to connect more to my roots. And that experience led me to see how important it is to connect with my tribe. The very earliest tribes were likely extended families...as I connected more with my family, I felt more connected to my tribe.

In this era of DNA testing and being able to pinpoint your ancestry, it's fun to consider where your roots are and how you are connected to those who came before you. The DNA of your ancestors lives on in you and as you discover your roots they connect you to your tribe.

For Reflection

What are your roots and what do they mean to you?

CHAPTER 14

Connection and Community

"The need for connection and community is
primal, as fundamental as the need for air,
water, and food."

—*Dean Ornish*

The past is never far away, especially the parts of our
past that make us who we are; I know I'm telling you
the following story to connect the dots of my past and
tie them into my future. It's what my soul has called
me to do.

I loved village and small-town life in Hungary. In the
small villages, you greet everyone that you see, and day-
to-day life is closely intertwined with your neighbors.

I think it's like this in villages and small towns all over the world.

I'm a city girl though, born and raised in Johannesburg, who moved to the very small town—although not quite a village—of Socorro, New Mexico, when I was ten years old. And not only was I born in a big city, I had many experiences of another big city on my trips to Budapest in Hungary. Even though I love the villages and small towns in Hungary, I am still drawn to the city of my heart, Budapest. I think about the people walking on the sidewalks; people packed into buses, trams, trolleys, and metro cars; long lines at the post office; and hordes of people moving through the streets, going about their business, moving among the stalls at outdoor markets, and surging into the metro cars from the crowded platforms. During peak tourist season the population of the city quadruples. The buzz and energy of so many people is exhilarating and it's an energy that propels me (and gives the city its pulsing heartbeat).

I used to see people I recognized from the villages in the city. Little old ladies dressed all in black, kerchiefs covering their heads, clutching small bouquets of flowers to sell at the metro stations. After the fall of communism, life became more difficult for populations that the State used to take care of. With the end of retirement benefits, seniors had to travel from their villages to Budapest to sell their wares to make extra money.

It is hard to pass by these women—their faces wrinkled by years of hard work, their hands gnarled by time—without buying something; my roommate often succumbed and so my apartment was regularly filled with the fragrance of many small bouquets of flowers.

Everyone knows everyone in the villages and small towns. During my visits when I was young, my grandfather would walk proudly through Balassagyarmat with me, showing me off to all his friends and neighbors. Even a short walk to the neighborhood market to buy milk and bread was an excursion filled with greetings and conversations. There, you're part of an extended family, a network that is rooted in centuries of tradition and a connection across generations.

There are "villages" in the city as well. Children who grow up in the same neighborhoods, raised in the same tall, grey, Communist-style block apartment buildings have community as well. They transition from elementary school to middle school and high school with one another and stay connected throughout the years. In the city it's easy to visit the other "villages" that exist, moving from district to district, and relationships can be forged, although not easily. City people are more guarded, they wear their city persona like the clothes they put on in the morning, using that persona to protect them from being overwhelmed by the three million other people living there.

Yet there is still a humanity and a connection with others in the city: I recall a young man jumping up from his seat on the bus to allow an elderly woman to sit down; a blue-collar worker asking a man who was legless, and on a small cart with wheels, if he needed help crossing the street, then picking him up and carrying him across the cobblestones; a businessman picking up one of the handles of a baby carriage that a young mother was struggling to maneuver down a long flight of stairs, sharing the load with her and helping her manage; a young woman buying a sandwich and giving it away to an elderly man who was begging for money.

Though city people wear their personas to protect themselves, their humanity is still there, just below the surface, ready to appear when a situation calls for it. You can sense this connectedness and you know the village is still there, still present, still living within the hearts of people. I was born with this notion of connectedness in my heart and whenever I found it lacking, wherever I was living at the time, I came to recognize that I needed to fill that gap. It was a drive within me to build more connection and to feel part of a tribe, even though I didn't always know that that's what I was trying to do. It was a longing in my heart and it seemed to be a driving force. How can people get connected in the midst of so much disconnect? This question is what drove and motivated me.

And I believe it exists in the hearts of people everywhere. Humans started out as small tribes of hunter-gatherers, typically not growing to more than 150 in a tribe. In *Tribes: We Need You to Lead Us,* author Seth Godin shares the concept that humans are wired to unite and form tribes. Godin defines a tribe as any group of people, large or small, who are connected to one another, a leader, and an idea. According to Godin, tribes are a powerful force of influence and change, thus professionals should learn to tap into the potential of forming and leading tribes. While Seth Godin's focus is on marketing and the power of the tribe to influence and exact change, he's brought this concept back into the spotlight after we'd "forgotten" about the importance of tribes.

Dave Logan, John King, and Halee Fischer-Wright state that "the success of a company depends on its tribes" in *Tribal Leadership: Leveraging Natural Groups to Build a Thriving Organization*. They share that the strength of an organization is determined by the tribal culture, and a thriving corporate culture can be established by an effective tribal leader. They describe how there are five stages in the development of tribal culture. The first of these stages is being "alienated" and the last stage is being a "team." The behavior they describe at each of the five stages in their model describes how mindsets can move from individualistic to a tribal culture.

In retrospect, one of my first managers was a tribal leader. Matthew Ellison had teams of young interns working for him. We would get together every morning to chat and to discuss the day. The focus was always on the team and working together to accomplish the vision of the organization. This togetherness was infused in the culture and we had a tremendous amount of support for one another as we often collaborated. We were invested in one another's lives; we were a tribe.

Having a tribal leader makes a huge difference in a work team. The leader sets the stage for how the team interacts and how they work with one another. The more "tribal" a leader is, the more likely that they create a tribe that works well together. The more successful teams I have encountered are definitely more tribal in nature.

This concept of tribes is not new, yet has gained momentum in many organizations today. And for good reason. When people are happy at work, when they are engaged, they are more productive, they have fewer sick days, and there is less drama and conflict in the workplace.

For Reflection

Do you agree with the quote at the beginning of this chapter? Why or why not?

CHAPTER 15

Facing Fear Is the Way Out

"Remember, we see the world not as it is but
as we are. Most of us see through the eyes
of our fears and our limiting beliefs and our
false assumptions."

—*Robin S. Sharma*

I n order to play bigger in the world, you have to face
and conquer your fears. Once you make a declaration—
"I want to make a powerful impact on the workplace and
change the culture of business"—your limiting beliefs
(the Gremlins, the Inner Critic, the negative thoughts)
can come creeping in. They can be hard to recognize

sometimes because these Gremlins or thoughts may mask themselves as good, common sense.

"Your idea is way too big. You need to scale it down."

"Who do you think YOU are to make an impact?"

"You're not successful enough to make a difference."

"This is going to take WAY too much time and energy."

I was sitting at my desk one day, working on my Tribal Abundance program. I had been wrestling with some of the feedback I had received and was trying to refine the content. Suddenly, an overwhelming feeling of exhaustion filled my body. It felt as though someone had pulled a plug and all the energy drained out of my body, like water draining from a sink. It felt like "too much." I was being asked to do too much, and the worst part of it was that I was the one doing the asking.

All these negative thoughts began to rush into my head and I could feel myself getting really angry with myself. "Who do you think you are?! Why can't you be satisfied with taking a job in an organization, continuing to build your career that way? Why do you think that you're so special that you have something unique to bring to the world?"

These thoughts bounced around in my head; it was like someone had let off a gunshot in a canyon that echoed and reverberated. I felt hopeless. My heart sank as I realized the amount of time, energy, and effort it was going to take for me to impact the world in the way my heart desired.

"Am I up for this?" I wondered. Thoughts of past failures and mistakes filled my head and I was sure that I had taken on too much.

"There is no way I'm going to succeed," I thought. And I began one of the most damaging and destructive practices (that we all do): I started to compare myself to others. I thought about the friends, colleagues, luminaries, and thought leaders that had achieved the kind of success I was hoping for. There was NO WAY that I could compare to any of them; no way could I achieve the kind of success and impact that they had achieved.

And then it was like a light bulb turned on; I had one of those aha moments. I recognized that I was falling into a destructive pattern that kept me from taking a risk, from gambling and betting it all.

I had used emotional freedom technique (EFT[1])—or tapping—in the past to help me stop repetitive and negative thought patterns, and I began to tap the center of my chest with two fingers. I had been taught that this is the anxiety spot and I knew that I needed to get myself out of that negative and anxious thought pattern.

Once I had settled down and taken a few deep breaths, I acknowledged that if all those other people could be successful, then there was no reason for *me* not to be.

Releasing myself from all the fears, insecurities, and anxiety helped me to shift my perspective and truly understand on a deep gut level—a spiritual level—that if I truly believed in an abundance mindset then my negative thoughts weren't in alignment with that. And I recognized how easy it was to let the fear take over, to be pulled along by insecurity like a leaf on a swiftly flowing river. That leaf has no control and is pulled this way and that by the current, going whichever way the water takes it.

But if someone sees that leaf and fishes it out of the water, it's no longer at the mercy of the current. And in the same way we need to pull those thoughts, those leaves, out of the currents of our minds to keep them from floating farther downstream. Having negative thoughts is a choice: we need to figure out how to choose the positive ones.

So how do you pull that leaf out of the river? The first step in making a shift is recognizing that you are having the negative thoughts in the first place. As I shared earlier, sometimes those thoughts mask themselves as common sense. But if you are having "not enough" thoughts—I'm not good enough, I'm not smart enough, I'm not pretty enough—it's definitely a good indication that you have slipped over to the Dark Side! Identifying the issue, in itself, helps you to shift your thinking. You then need to replace those negative thoughts with positive ones. The positive thoughts should be statements that really resonate with you, and should be phrased in the present tense. For example, if you have the negative thought, "I'm not smart enough" running through your mind, every time you become aware of that thought stop, take a deep breath, and say, "I am a smart and creative person." And then say it again. And to ramp up the effect, look at yourself in the mirror while you're doing it.

Here's an important tip: even if right now you *don't believe* the positive thought, say it anyway. And keep saying it. And the beautiful thing is that just like those simple wellness practices you do (e.g., drinking water, taking walks, eating a balanced diet, meditation, prayer) as you keep doing it you will see the results. You will come to believe the positive thoughts as true—and they are—and the negative thoughts will decrease.

One final thing about shifting your mindset to be more positive: surround yourself with positive people— find your tribe. You've probably heard the quote that is attributed to Jim Rohn, "You're the average of the five people you spend the most time with." There's even a research study, the Framingham Heart Study (a social network research study), that shows having happy friends makes *you* happier. So, as you focus on releasing the negative thoughts, begin to think about how you can bring more positive people into your tribe. (Because of the importance of the concept of negative thoughts, also termed "limiting beliefs," we'll come back to this in Chapter 29.)

For Reflection

What steps are you going to take to begin to shift your thinking?

CHAPTER 16

Foundational Framework

"Where can we go to find God if we cannot see Him in our own hearts and in every living being?"

—*Swami Vivekananda*

Love. Connection. Being together. Harmony. Laughter. Joy.

When I think about what my worldview is, these are the words that come to mind. I truly do see people as connected, all as one. Maybe it's because I've lived and experienced so many different cultures that I automatically look for the common threads: what are the things that connect us all? What is it that we as the human race have in common?

I grew up going to a traditional church and we attended as a family every Sunday. It was part of who I was as a person, although my concept of God was a bit fuzzy. He seemed to me to be a stern grandfather who had a lot of rules that had to be followed. And yet there were the holidays: chocolate eggs and bright new dresses on Easter, presents and a tree for Christmas. The ritual of church and celebrating holidays set the foundation in me for a belief in God and all things spiritual, yet religion was not something I was strongly connected to.

When I started working part-time at KFC and was sometimes scheduled to work on Sunday mornings, it gave me a sense of freedom, almost a sense that I was doing something wrong, to not attend church, but it was deliciously wrong, something I still wanted to do. It was very freeing and exhilarating and I dismissed the negative reaction of my father on those days. He was very traditional and going to church as a family was important to him. My father treasured the rituals of us all getting ready on Sunday mornings, putting on our best clothes, and then driving together as a family to the church service. He would look with pride on his family—his beautiful wife, two sons and daughter—and that pride spilled over into his understanding of tradition, God's blessing, and culture. For my father, it wasn't so much about his faith as it was about a ritual that connected him to others, to the family he had to leave behind in Hungary, and to the culture that lived in him but that was not part of his world.

But, for me as a teenager, wanting to find my own way and discover my own path, having "permission" to skip church and go to work instead was freeing.

Later in college, I became involved with an evangelical Christian ministry and further left behind the traditions of my roots. I grew up with the rituals and traditions of the Catholic church; the atmosphere was hushed and serious. As a family we would solemnly file down the center aisle of the church, genuflecting before entering our pew. We sat quietly, communicating only if necessary in a quiet whisper.

I can remember walking into Calvary Chapel for the first time. I was there with a friend, a sorority sister, and I can remember the sensation of freedom that I felt. The church was housed in a large building, the main sanctuary was a former indoor soccer field and the floors were bare. Simple metal folding chairs covered the concrete floors in rows and there was a buzz in the air, the sound of people talking and laughing. It felt so incredibly alive and the energy and excitement and casual atmosphere was a sharp contrast to the quiet, solemn, whispered hush of the churches of my youth. I felt more alive and excited and connected—to God, to others—in this place.

Then the guitars, drums, and piano began to play and my heart stirred. Voices rose all around me as people began to worship their God with song. A feeling of love and joy filled me and I knew I had found my church home.

The service was still about God, but there was a sense of openness and freedom when compared to what I had learned about God and church as a young child. I was able to let go of the guilt and ritual and embraced things like *grace, forgiveness, love.* These were part of my traditional Catholic upbringing, but were cloaked in thousands of years of tradition and my heart yearned to find my own path to discovering what these words truly meant.

After a simple prayer said in my dorm room (my first semester of college), I was "in." I had joined others who yearned for the unconditional love of a God who sacrificed his Son so that people could have fellowship with Him.

While God's love is unconditional, his people's love is not always. While his people accepted his forgiveness and grace, it was harder for those same people to extend grace and forgiveness *to* others. That was my challenge, too. I recognized that coming from a place of judgment rather than from a place of acceptance was constraining me. It was squeezing my heart and the judgment I had for people was limiting me from being open to everyone. It had felt as though I wasn't connected enough to the world and had been hiding in a Christian sub-culture where the rules were clear and everything was viewed in black and white. That didn't fit anymore; I felt as though everything around me was in shades of grey and I needed to release my hold on absolutes.

When Jesus was asked by a Pharisee, "What is the greatest commandment?" He responded that it was love: to love God and love others. And this eventually became my "religion," to love God and love others and not pay attention to what I was told was "sin" and would separate me and others from God. Wasn't the whole point of Christ sacrificing himself on the cross to bridge that gap between sinful man and God? The focus had seemed to me to instead become living a sinless life—each and every "sin" was something to avoid, to hide. And so, the community of love that was originally based upon forgiveness and grace had become, to me, a community where people were asked instead to put on masks of "perfection" to hide their sins and flaws. How could I continue to live a life like that, one that did not feel authentic?

While love and connection is still very much a piece of who I am, my understanding of and relationship with God has transformed and evolved and shifted. God has become too big for me to box into specific practices or to understand from the pages of a book—God is in each one of us and connects us to all, and that connection is through love.

When I was in high school I read a book by Wayne Dyer, *Your Erroneous Zones*. I have no idea how I got the book, although I suspect it was accidentally purchased at a garage sale when I misread the title. I thought it said "erogenous" zones and as a teenager that sounded super interesting to me!

I devoured the book. It opened up new worlds and new ideas, all based on one simple premise: you have a choice. There were so many things in my life in which I felt I had no choice: where we lived (Socorro, not Johannesburg), what I looked like, my family, my name, the list went on. At a time in my life when I felt unsure, insecure, vulnerable, and afraid, this book was like a beacon in the night, a lighthouse, calling me to safe shores. I could give up my tossing and bobbing around like a boat on choppy waves, and being pulled under in the turbulent waters of my life, and instead set sail towards the safe shore by focusing on the light that guided me.

The lessons from the book permeated every fiber of my being and I began to release negative and unhealthy patterns of thinking and embrace the ability to control my feelings and reactions. I think this is when I first began to live the principles of Tribal Abundance, even though the concept had not yet been developed. I started to recognize how my thoughts could be "wrong," and that how I chose to think about things could affect the way I lived my life. I was already very aware of my need for connection—the tribal piece—and this was really my first introduction to the abundance piece, to reframing my thoughts and living with the perspective that there was no lack. I learned that some of the erroneous beliefs I had were like bars in a prison cell, keeping me trapped. And as I began to release those thoughts and practiced living out the opposite of those thoughts, the bars slowly fell away, one by one, and I was free.

For Reflection

What is your understanding of a higher power? Do your thoughts sometimes lead you to misperceive instances in your life?

THE PROGRAM

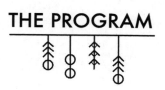

CHAPTER 17

Tribal Abundance — The Start of a Better Way

"Every new beginning comes from some other beginning's end."

—*Seneca*

"**Y**ou have to be a thought leader!" These words resonated through my mind and it was as though every cell in my body said, "Yes!" I had begun to see patterns and similarities in the work I was doing in organizations and with my individual coaching clients. There were issues and problems that seemed to be common to all, and my heart yearned to be able to help. The desire deep within me, formed and developed by my experiences and shaped by my journey, to help others to find their place and to live a connected and full life led to the birth of Tribal Abundance.

The woman who spoke the words about being a thought leader presented her work to my local coaching chapter through a virtual program. It was in early 2016, and the focus of my consulting business had shifted to include coaching. Because the words resonated so deeply with me, I wanted to work with her and took her up on her offer of a free session. During that session—while I could tell she was in "sales" mode—I could begin to see the sun peeking through the clouds around the idea of thought leadership. She explained that she used a process to get me to think through the work I do and to help me discover what it is that sets me apart; the goal was to help me stand out from the pack. I decided to hire her and we scheduled our first official call.

It was not a comfortable process. That first session, I got a queasy feeling in my gut, and I felt butterflies. My heart rate increased and all I could hear was the sound of my heartbeat; it was so loud in my head that I imagined even my coach could hear it. My mouth went dry and I desperately had to swallow; so I kept swallowing, hoping it would help. I felt like a wild animal that had been trapped and I kept looking for a way out. Despite the discomfort of that first session, I had committed to working with her and knew that I could not give up.

During each subsequent session, my coach would question me and then question me more, always trying to dig deeper, to get to the core of why I was doing what I did, what it was that propelled me in the work I had chosen to do. I can remember feeling so irritated. I was being asked all these questions and I felt inadequate in my answers. "I've completed coach training," I thought. "We were taught that it's all about the client, NOT about the coach and that we're NOT supposed to influence our client's decisions!" I thought the questions I was being asked were very leading and it made me feel as though the answers I was giving were somehow wrong. Some sessions felt so uncomfortable that I would literally squirm in my seat and my heart would race. Sometimes, I could feel the irritation rising in me, my face getting warm, and I felt as though I was going to explode. I bit back the words I wanted to say. I felt diminished, as though my opinions and experiences weren't good enough somehow.

After that first painful phone call things got a little bit easier. Eventually, I was finally able to take a step back and recognize what my coach wanted me to do: she wanted me to create something that was completely original and completely my own, based on how I worked with my clients. She was like a cook experimenting in a kitchen, mixing different things together, adding a bit of this and that, stirring, adding something else, pouring some of the mixture out and discarding it. The "ingredients" she was adding and discarding each time were my experiences and emotions and I felt vulnerable. Raw. Scared.

"What the hell have I done?" I thought. I'd committed myself to a painful process and I wasn't sure I even LIKED my coach anymore. I had invested in the process—with both my time and my money—and I had no idea if it was going to be worth it.

I now recognize these pains as those that my potential clients have. "Who is this Ildi person and how does what she has to offer bring me value?" I can imagine these questions in the minds of people as they wonder what the heck it is they've gotten themselves into. "Tribal Abundance? What does that even MEAN?" And as they go through the process, the emotions come up, the fears, the anger, the frustration, the irritation. How could I ask my clients to experience this if it wasn't something I was willing to do as well?

I talked about my career and work life, and I shared about the experiences—good and bad—that had shaped me. I spoke about my passion for people and my desire for connection. She continued to dig and dig, like someone searching for buried treasure, knowing that it was there and that it just needed to be unearthed.

And with persistence, she found it. The treasure—buried deep between layers of stories and experiences, joys and pains, hopes and discouragements, and memories—was there all along, and it had a heart that beat with the sounds of my childhood.

For Reflection

What are some of the new beginnings you've embarked on? Were they painful?

CHAPTER 18

Learning Life Lessons

"We all learn lessons in life. Some stick, some don't. I have always learned more from rejection and failure than from acceptance and success."

—*Henry Rollins*

When I had my Lucy Moment—when I first learned that there are external things that affect how we interact with one another—the pain, guilt, and shame I felt as a little girl deeply affected me and affected how I interacted with others from that day forward. It was a lesson I learned again and again through my life:

people are more than their appearance, their physical beauty, the color of their skin. Yet at the same time I was strongly influenced by the culture I grew up in that worshipped physical beauty as a god. It meant power, prestige.

I try to imagine what Lucy is doing now. She most likely had a life very different from mine. A much harder life. One in which the color of her skin kept her from having the opportunities I had. And in apartheid-era South Africa, she wasn't even considered a whole person. She became to me an icon of those who, at the time, were viewed as something less than human. They had no respect for her or for her dreams and hopes, desires and ambitions. There were very few options for work, one of which was to work for a very low wage cleaning someone's house.

Back in my sophomore year of college, I enjoyed being in the Greek system. All I had known of fraternities and sororities came from television and movies and I was reluctant to get involved in one. But I took a risk and pledged a sorority the second semester of college along with two good friends from high school. There were parties and activities and boys! The house right across from ours was the Alpha Tau Omega (ATO) house. My sorority sisters and I would spend time over there, hanging with the fraternity guys. We made good friends and I remember a lot of laughter.

One weekend they had a few guys visiting from another chapter. They were from another university and were probably there for a football game or other sporting event. There was one in particular whose company I really enjoyed. He had an easy way about him, turning everything into a joke, and my friend Debbie and I were doubled over with laughter the whole evening, gasping for breath at the wildly funny things he said. It was light and fun and free and I remember feeling so happy and content. "THIS is what college life is about!" I thought. I was enjoying my life and enjoying the company of those I was with.

The next evening when we went back, I could physically sense a huge shift in the atmosphere. Whereas the evening before, I had felt welcome and enjoyed the camaraderie of the ATOs, stepping into the house on that night, I felt a coldness, an unwelcoming atmosphere. My buddy from the night before turned a cold stare towards me. I tried to joke and laugh with him as we'd done the night before but he froze me out. He would barely look at me. I had no idea what changed but I felt so rejected; a cold, icy feeling rose in my chest and I couldn't breathe. I felt awkward and ungainly, everything about me felt wrong. I started to panic and thought, "I have to get out here!" I felt an icy knot of fear develop in my stomach; I felt unsafe and needed to escape. (Yep, I needed to seek refuge.)

Many hours after I had left, I was sitting in my room, allowing the icy coldness to fill me and seep out through my eyes via tears filled with hurt and rejection, wondering what was wrong with me and why I had been rejected. My friend Debbie finally found me. I asked her, "What did I do wrong?" She had noticed how the room had shifted against me as well, and how our new friend had suddenly rejected me; she had stayed when I left.

"He found out that you were from South Africa," she told me.

I was floored. What difference did that make? Yes, he was African American, a black man, and so he knew very well what was happening in that part of the world to people whose skin was the same as his.

"I didn't choose where I was born!" I cried out. I couldn't understand how something I had no control over made me a pariah and made me someone to be shunned and rejected.

It wasn't until many years later that I made the connection. Just as he had rejected me based on where I was born without taking into account who I was as a person, he had likely been shunned and rejected based on the color of his skin without taking into account who HE was as a person. I represented to him the country that had the most oppressive laws in the world for people of color, and in his identification with them, I was the enemy.

Our conversation had never touched on the topic of his experience as a black man in the US, but from what I've learned from my friends of color since is that prejudice is always just under the surface. It's something that is part of everyday existence and affects every experience a person of color has.

Although it was a painful experience for me to be rejected and disliked for something over which I had no control—a Lucy Moment—it gave me some insight into the topic of race and how it is played out in this country and others. There are humans who experience rejection and dislike based on the color of their skin. It's not fair, they have no choice in the matter, and there's nothing they can (or should) do about the color of their skin.

This was yet another experience that created in me that desire for something more: I can envision tribes of people of all shapes, colors, and sizes where the focus is not on what differentiates, but rather is on the collaboration that is magical because of the diversity of the tribe people's backgrounds and experiences. I know how important it is for differing perspectives and ideas to be allowed to flourish together in order to co-create something completely new. It's exactly why we're warned about "groupthink" and about how damaging that can be to creativity, innovation, and even safety.

One of the biggest lessons for me in a cross-cultural awareness class I took years ago was the principle of "it's not wrong, it's just different." This is a big shift from all-or-nothing thinking to more nuanced, critical thinking. I love how Margaret Heffernan talks about this principle in *Willful Blindness: Why We Ignore the Obvious at Our Peril* and how our brains naturally think in polarities. We have to work to think more critically and allow for perspectives that are not absolutes.

There is something in the human brain/experience that can make us unwilling to take the risk of thinking new thoughts and looking at things from another perspective. We may succumb to that base, primal urge to be "safe" and end up shortchanging ourselves on life. To keep us safe, our brains seem to make us naturally gravitate to those who look like us and think like us. But it's actually dangerous to go too far in that direction because taking this to the extreme, you have racist, narrow-minded people who think that everything different is wrong. It's essential to step out of our comfort zones and cross the boundaries of color, religion, political beliefs, and socio-economic status. It's only when we truly try to see things from another person's perspective that we increase our capacity for empathy and become more connected to those around us.

For Reflection

What are some of the difficult lessons you've had to learn from being misjudged by others? Do you tend to gravitate to those like yourself?

CHAPTER 19

The Tribal Abundance Model

"Alone we can do so little; together we can do so much."

—*Helen Keller*

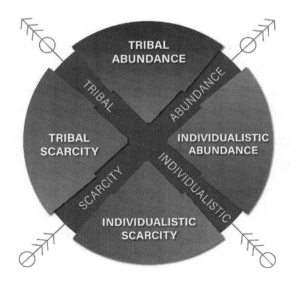

When I first launched my program, I reached out to colleagues I trust and respect to get their input. I invited them to a full-day workshop that would highlight the concept of Tribal Abundance and shared that I was interested in their feedback on the experience. I was very clear that this was going to be a collaborative approach, that I was interested in their thoughts on their experience. Here is what I sent:

Dear Barbra —

Hope you are doing well!

I'm very excited about a project I've been working on lately—my Tribal Abundance® program. I've developed this program to help teams and organizations change their culture from one of scarcity to abundance by creating a tribal culture in an organization. It's based on the work of the anthropologist Dr. Colin Turnbull.

To share the concept, I'm hosting a Tribal Abundance Experience on Friday, January 27th. During this unique and interactive workshop, I'll be sharing concepts of the program, and asking for YOUR feedback to help me refine the workshop and market it to those who need it most.

You are invited to this free, all-day workshop ($497 value) because you are someone whose opinion is important to me. Please click "reply" by Dec 9th and let me know

if you're coming – there is a limited number of spots.
   I hope you can make it!

Best,
Ildi

I was nervous. It felt as though I was taking a really big step, one that took a lot of courage. In a way, I was baring my soul to them, which felt a little bit scary. And yet, after the workshop I was overwhelmed by the positive responses, the constructive feedback, and the testimonials I received. Years of thoughts, concepts, dreams, and hard work were finally validated. Tribal Abundance had arrived.

***

The model really looks at two continuums: (1) tribal versus individualistic, and (2) abundance versus scarcity. Let's look at the first continuum, tribal versus individualistic.

As you have read, throughout my journey I've always been drawn to connection and collaboration. That is the tribal piece. Think again of the BaMbuti tribe versus the Ik tribe: the BaMbuti thrived by collaborating and inter-weaving their lives. Remember the principles that they lived by: working together, hunting together, everyone participates and everyone benefits no matter their role, cooperation is key, trusting that the forest will provide for them, connection to the forest in a spiritual way, clear expectations of behavior, being grateful and giving thanks, and putting the good of the whole above the good of the self. In contrast, the Ik focused very much on themselves as individuals and thus they did not thrive.

I think this concept of tribalism can be challenging in modern western culture where we tend to be more individualistic. I think of the pioneer spirit here in the United States and how that desire to strike out on one's own and make a new life was the foundation for this country's development. In many ways we've gone to an extreme with individualism and thus we have sacrificed the tribal piece.

I remember sharing this principle in a workshop one day recently, and two of the participants said that this was a really hard concept for them. "We're business students!" they laughed, "Everything we are learning is based on the model of competition!" Perhaps the time has come for business schools to update some of their teachings.

In today's workplace in the US there is a tremendous focus on competition and the workplace is generally viewed as a zero-sum game: there are winners, and there are losers. While there are books out there about how competition is healthy and can help performance, (e.g., *Top Dog: The Science of Winning and Losing*) increasingly, there is a new focus on collaboration as a way to work.

In Margaret Heffernan's book, *A Bigger Prize: How We Can Do Better than the Competition,* she challenges the assumption of competition being the better way. She describes how competition regularly produces rising levels of fraud, cheating, stress, inequality, and political stalemate. She writes about siblings who won't speak to each other, children who burn out at school, the proliferation of doping among athletes, and how auditors and fund managers go to jail for insider trading.

Her premise is that individuals and organizations can find supportive and creative ways to collaborate and work together. She believes that the future belongs to people and companies who work together rather than against one another, and the research she has conducted supports this premise. It's not the star employee who outperforms everyone that drives the most high-achieving teams, it's social cohesion—where team members ask one another for help—that leads to greater results. This is a radically different approach to what drives people to do their best work and what it means to be a leader.

In the book *Give and Take,* author Adam Grant shares how, for many generations, the focus has been on the individual drivers of success: passion, hard work, talent, and luck. However, he notes that today, success is increasingly dependent on how people interact with one other. He identified the styles of "giving," "taking," and "matching" that characterize how people typically operate while at work. Each one of these styles has a surprising impact on success. His research shows that, although some of the others-focused *givers* are exploited and burn out, many givers achieve extraordinary results across a wide range of industries. Surprisingly, it's not the *takers,* those who are fixated on always getting more than they give, who will be most successful. They are the ones with a competitive mindset who operate in a way in which they want to extract as much as possible from others and never get taken advantage of. But they are not the most successful.

And it's not the *matchers* either, those who believe in quid pro quo, who are most successful. Matchers are extremely attuned to fairness and perceived equality in relationships. If they do you a favor, they expect one in return and will feel indebted to you if they're on the receiving end of a good deed. They give, but do it while keeping score. This in in contrast with the givers who simply seek to enrich the lives of the people they interact with. As Grant writes, "If you're a giver . . . you simply strive to be generous in sharing your time, energy, knowledge, skills, ideas, and connections with other people who can benefit from them."

Both of these research-based books show that there *is* another way. It doesn't have to be pure competition where there is a winner and a loser. What about collaboration and co-creating, coming up with something that benefits everyone? When it comes to sports competitions and athletic events, healthy competition is good and yes, there is a clear winner. But the purpose of sports is for entertainment and they are not going to bring about new technologies that increase efficiency or new research that brings hope and healing to the sick. Sports play a very important role in our lives and are of great value, but operating a business on the winner-loser competitive-sports paradigm is clearly not the most successful way for positive long-term results.

Incidentally, there is definitely a tribal piece to team sports. For the team to succeed, members need to depend on one another and each needs to contribute their unique skills. Not all competition is bad, but consider it on a continuum—collaboration is more tribal and competition is more individualistic—and in an appropriate environment.

In fact, in the January 2013 online article "Collaboration is the New Competition," in the *Harvard Business Review,* Ben Hecht writes about the growing trend called collective impact. The complex and interconnected problems that leaders and organizations are facing today can't be addressed by individual efforts, and they are putting aside self-interest and are collaborating using the collective impact framework. Collaboration is not a new concept, but individuals are coming together and embracing a new way of working together to solve problems.

For example, I worked with an organization that wanted to revamp its customer service training. The organization had identified inconsistencies in the customer service experience based on the data they collected from surveys of current customers. The project owner and I agreed that bringing together diverse voices from across all divisions and departments in the organization was key, both in getting different perspectives as well as creating buy-in. We pulled together a team of people that, based on the size of the organization, didn't even know one another.

Psychologist and professor Bruce Tuckman developed a group development model in 1963 that is helpful in understanding how to help a team work together. There are four phases: Forming, Storming, Norming, and Performing. Naturally we wanted the team we had put together to get to the performing stage as quickly as possible. It was important that our team focus on collaboration and sharing, and not spend time competing with one another (which can potentially happen during the storming phase).

In order to facilitate collaboration, we co-created the performance goals, the process we would follow, as well as our communication plan. I had a framework for the group to follow to ensure that we kept on track, and during our weekly project update meetings we would check in on where we were. As the weeks progressed I could see the trust increasing and more openness and sharing. We had established Ground Rules as a group at the beginning and would post these at each meeting. The ground rules were very simple and included things like, show up on time, be prepared, no interrupting, think before speaking, etc. These ground rules kept the group work respectful.

Through collaboration, the disparate team we brought together created a new training program that not only helped to move the needle in a positive direction when it came to their customers' perceptions of their customer service experience, it was also an award-winning project. Without collaboration there is no way that we could have accomplished all that we did. And that company now enjoys a vastly improved experience.

For Reflection

What do you think is the best part about collaborating with others? What are the challenges?

CHAPTER 20

Abundance vs. Scarcity Mindset

"I have an abundance mentality: When people are genuinely happy at the successes of others, the pie gets larger."

—*Stephen Covey*

The second continuum of the Tribal Abundance model is abundance versus scarcity. Not enough jobs, not enough money, not enough funding: not enough. This is scarcity-mindset thinking. Someone with a scarcity mindset typically thinks in terms of shortages and savings, of keeping resources to themselves. They have a mentality which promotes individual selfishness over collective good. Those with an abundance mindset think in terms of collective solutions and collaboration, and they encourage creativity and foster a culture of high performance. They think, "What if?" and "Why not?"

Although Steven Covey's book, *The 7 Habits of Highly Effective People: Powerful Lessons in Personal Change* was published in 1989, it wasn't until a few years later that I was exposed to it for the first time. Just before I moved overseas to Hungary in the early nineties, I went through International Team's training program in Prospect Heights, Illinois. My favorite part of the training was the cross-cultural class and I loved the principles and theories we learned about that were in alignment with how I had lived my life. I especially loved learning the principle of "it's not wrong, it's just different." It was in this class that I first learned about Steven Covey and his book.

The idea of abundance mentality or abundance mindset was first identified in Covey's book. He writes that an abundance mindset is one in which a person believes there are enough resources and successes to share with others. That mindset was contrasted with the scarcity mindset which is when people believe that there is not enough, there are limited resources and not enough to go around. The takers discussed earlier, from Adam Grant's *Give and Take,* are a good example of those with a scarcity mindset as they think that if someone else wins or is successful in a situation, that means all others lose. Individuals with an abundance mindset, on the other hand, are able to reject the concept of zero-sum games and can celebrate the success of others rather than feel threatened by it.

I can remember when Steven Covey's *The 7 Habits of Highly Effective People: Powerful Lessons in Personal Change* became the language of the workplace. All of a sudden people were focusing on habits to make themselves better people and were positively impacting the workforce.

Covey believes that an abundance mindset comes from having a high self-worth and security. There is such a sharp contrast in doing business with someone who comes from an abundance perspective versus someone who comes from a scarcity perspective. I used to come from a scarcity mindset where I didn't believe that there was enough love, talent, opportunity, fill-in-the-blank to go around. It felt as though everything I did was driven by fear and that caused me to be someone who tried to grasp at things, wanting to hold on tightly to them, because I felt if I let go I would lose those things. And those "things" could be friendships, opportunities, money, material objectives, admiration from others, just about anything. But once my mindset began to shift to abundance—which takes a lifetime; it's a journey I'm still on today—I noticed that I was living with less fear.

When you live in fear, your body goes through neurological and physiological responses that can affect every aspect of your life. Your heart rate increases, your blood pressure goes up, your breathing gets faster, and adrenaline and cortisol are released. The release of adrenaline also increases your blood pressure, expands the air passages of the lungs, which is why it may sometimes feel more difficult to breathe, and pushes the blood to your muscles. Cortisol floods the body with glucose, which supplies large muscles with an immediate energy source…then it inhibits insulin. It narrows the arteries and with the increase in heart rate the blood is forced to pump harder and faster. This is what fear feels like!

When you're operating from an abundance mindset, you experience the exact opposite: your heart beats at a regular rate, your blood pressure normalizes, you experience normal breathing patterns, and your body releases the "feel good" and calming hormones of dopamine and oxytocin. Operating from this place allows you to share profits, recognition, and responsibility without feeling as though you are losing or being taken advantage of.

What makes a person generous? The answer is

believing in abundance. However, we misunderstand abundance if we think of it in terms of "having a lot." In fact, as Ken Stern of *The Atlantic* reported in March 2013, "One of the most surprising, and perhaps confounding, facts of charity in America is that the people who can least afford to give are the ones who donate the greatest percentage of their income." On average, the wealthiest 20% of Americans (those with annual earnings in the top one-fifth of the population) gave 1.3% of their incomes to charity in 2011. In comparison, Americans whose incomes placed them in the bottom 20% of the country donated 3.2% of their income during the same year.

If abundance doesn't come from financial wealth, then what's its source? Abundance is first and foremost an attitude about life. It's intimately connected to how we approach relationships. Think about the emotion of jealousy—it's a good indication that there is NOT an abundance mindset. Rather, a fear-based scarcity mindset is in play when one experiences jealousy.

I remember an ex-boyfriend being the jealous type. The first time he got angry that I was getting attention from other men I felt a little thrill. "He must really love me if he's jealous," I thought. What I didn't realize at the time was that my view of love was skewed (Isn't everyone's view of love skewed to some degree?) and that I would soon grow to hate and feel constrained by those jealous fits.

The jealousy he felt came from a place of scarcity; he seemed to feel that the love and attention I gave to and received from others somehow took away from the love and attention I would give to him as though there were a finite amount of love. Not only was he jealous of the attention men paid to me—and in all honesty it was nothing more than friendliness or possibly mild flirting—he was also jealous of the time I spent with friends and even of the time I spent focused on volunteer activities. I had assured him that I was a monogamous person and that I was in a relationship with HIM but this did not seem to address the issue of his jealousy. Clearly this was NOT a healthy relationship. But it took me awhile to recognize this and in reflecting back on those years with him, it actually helped me in future relationships because I recognized that I could never be with someone who was jealous, who came from a place of fear and scarcity.

When I met the man who later became my husband, it was his lack of jealousy that confirmed he was the right person for me. I was free to be the extroverted social butterfly I was born to be—talking and laughing with men and women—and it didn't faze him one bit. And that's really when I recognized how freeing an abundance mindset is, and how damaging, constraining, and unhealthy a scarcity mindset is in a relationship. Finally, I had the freedom to give and receive love and friendship without someone believing all of my love would be used up on others and there would be no more left for him. My husband believes, as I do, that love multiplies: the more we give and receive love, the more love we have to give and the greater capacity we have to receive love.

Growing up with two brothers, the three of us would always try to divvy things up and share fairly. If one of us thought that another of us had gotten more than their fair share, there was trouble! We would run to my parents and complain about it not being fair and they would have to manage the whole negotiation and mediation process to restore peace to the family. And having an uneven number of children made it even more of a challenge to divide things fairly. We were definitely operating more from the taker and matcher perspectives than that of giver.

I believe it's somehow ingrained in us to seek equity and fairness, but that's not necessarily the way the world works. I can remember crying, "It's not fair!" about so many things as a child, and it was only as an adult that I came to the realization that there is no guarantee of equity or fairness. And that's okay, especially if we are living with an abundance mindset. Releasing that expectation of equity and fairness is one of the first steps in developing an abundance mindset. (Keep in mind that "equity" and "fairness" are different concepts than "justice.")

The scarcity mindset term was coined by Sendhil Mullainathan, a Harvard economist, and Eldar Shafir, a Princeton psychologist. In *A Bigger Prize: Why Competition Isn't Everything and How We Do Better* Margaret Heffernan shares how they have documented the degree to which a scarcity mindset creates tunnel vision, which narrows perspective and shortens time horizons. Mullainathan and Shafir argue that the anxiety provoked by this sense of scarcity is enough to lower an individual's IQ by as much as losing a night's sleep can! (And losing a night's sleep is actually *worse than being over the legal alcohol limit* in terms of lowering an individual's IQ.)

Margaret Heffernan also shared that all social systems have some kind of hierarchy. Think of a hierarchy as a triangle where at the base of the triangle there is the least amount of power, status, and influence and the top of the triangle has the most. A hierarchy can be a very steep triangle (meaning that there are greater differentials in power, status, and influence from the bottom to the top) or a relatively flat triangle (which is more egalitarian and means there is less difference between the top and bottom levels). The steepness of the hierarchy has been termed the "power-distance index," as developed by Dutch social psychologist Geert Hofstede.

She writes that in countries with a high power-distance index, wealth, power, skills, and status go together and the powerful enjoy great privilege and often come from the same families. These types of societies are often characterized by economic inequality and the exercise of power depends on social or financial dominance. As she eloquently states, "You can describe a great deal about a culture—whether of a company or a country—by observing the distance between the powerful and the powerless. That distance always carries a cost, and the greater their distance the higher the social cost."

That social cost was reflected to me in the power-distance that existed in apartheid-era South Africa. It is illustrated by my Lucy Moment when I was living in a country whose whole philosophy was based on scarcity. The power-distance index was incredibly high and two young girls were caught and crushed in that hierarchy. Why would anyone want to live in scarcity and fear when they could live in abundance and endless possibility? How much more successful could we be as individuals, work teams, departments, organizations, companies, cities, and countries if we did not allow ourselves to be limited by lack and the fear of not enough, but instead, we embraced endless possibility and the concept of more?

In the article *What Scarcity and Abundance Mean to Your Career* by Ann Latham on Forbes.com, she shares that one with a scarcity mindset sees limitations instead of opportunities and because of that, shortages will prevail and everything becomes something to hoard or fight over because "there will never be enough."[2] Those living with a scarcity mindset see life as unfair and change as impossible. In contrast, the abundance mindset believes there is always more—more opportunities, more ideas to try, more places to explore, more ways to grow, more things to fall in love with, and more ways to turn a bad situation into a success.

My hope is that this concept of an abundance mindset—and the philosophy of Tribal Abundance—takes root in your heart and begins to grow and flourish like a well-loved plant. I believe that when society begins to look at things from this perspective, there will be a shift in a positive direction. And thinking of how that might play out in individuals' lives and in the workplace is exciting to me. I see people having honest and authentic conversations and addressing issues. I see an increased willingness to share ideas and resources and to collaborate. I see those collaborations happening more frequently, and people not worrying that someone is going to steal or take credit for their ideas. I see individuals giving one another encouragement and recognition, being confident that the success of the group is more important than the success of any one individual. I see engaged employees who are happy at work and performing their best, longing to make a positive difference in the world by being the best version of themselves they can be. I see people and companies thriving and succeeding without burnout and without sacrificing their values. I see it so clearly. Do you?

For Reflection

What does abundance mean to you? Can you identify ways in which you operate from a scarcity mindset?

CHAPTER 21

Tribal Culture vs. Individualistic Culture

"I think we have a lot to learn from ancient
cultures and different tribes."

—*Baron Vaughn*

In individualistic cultures, people are seen as independent and autonomous. Social behavior tends to be dictated by the attitudes and preferences of individuals and the health of the group as a whole is not the focus. Characteristics that are rewarded are strength, self-reliance, assertiveness, and independence. American culture is well known for being highly individualistic. We honor and appreciate the individual who has pulled him or herself up by the bootstraps and has become successful. We believe in the American Dream where the individual is not bound by their class or background and can be "successful." Success can be defined in different ways, but in American culture it is often defined as achieving wealth, respect, fame, or power. I love the concept of the American Dream yet I do believe that those strong individuals who rise like cream to the top didn't necessarily make it alone.

This contrasts with collectivistic cultures where characteristics like being self-sacrificing, dependable, generous, and helpful to others are of greater importance. This isn't about judging cultures and stating that more individualistic cultures are bad while more collectivistic cultures are good. Remember the lesson I learned in my cultural awareness class: it's not wrong, it's just different. In the very marrow of my bones beats the rhythm of a tribal drum. I can love being independent and self-sufficient and at the same time recognize that I need my tribe, that I need to be with my clan, my people.

And this is why my heart is Hungarian. I can connect with the way of life inside the small Hungarian villages and honor the way lives are interconnected. I can carry that village lifestyle inside my heart no matter where I go, and I can create a tribe in a large city simply by tapping into that spirit and connecting with like-minded people. I believe our very DNA carries that beat of the tribal drum, urging us to dance in the timeless tempo of the tribe.

There's something about connection that is vitally important to our mental and emotional health as humans. We've been wired with tribal-ness in our DNA, and we function best when we're with people. "But I'm an introvert!" or "I hate people!" you might say, thinking that you definitely do *not* function best when you're with other people. (And believe it or not, I've heard lots of people say they hate people.) Let's take a look at those two thoughts.

"I'm an introvert"—the whole concept of introversion and extroversion has to do with where a person gets their energy. And yes, an introvert can be drained by too much social interaction. But even the most introverted introvert needs some degree of social interaction; we are social creatures after all. Introverts are energized more by the internal world of thoughts and feelings; they tend to be more reserved and introspective. But it doesn't mean that they are shy or lack social skills. They just need more time alone to get energized. As humans we are wired to receive love and affection and even if introverts have a smaller circle of support, there is still a need for connection with others.

"I hate people"—when I hear this comment my first thought is that it is such a blanket statement there is no way it can be true! Does this mean that a person who feels this way hates all people all the time? What about family and friends? Are they hated as well? I often think that this is a *response* to the ugly and unkind behaviors of people in their experience. For example, when I hear news stories of people who have abused children or animals my gut reaction is one of horror and anger; I could easily say that I hate those people. But I don't really. I hate what they've done…abuse is often part of a cycle. I try to follow Covey's principle from *The 7 Habits of Highly Effective People: Powerful Lessons in Personal Change* of "seek first to understand, then to be understood."

There's a continuum from feeling a little blue to clinical depression, and each one of us has experienced depression to some degree. One of the negative consequences of a very individualistic society is depression. I'm gifted with the genetic makeup of a naturally optimistic nature that keeps me from suffering from depression. But that doesn't mean that I haven't felt sad and blue, and there are many people who are dear to me who suffer from anxiety and depression. I can remember a friend of mine explaining to me what a panic attack felt like and she described the feeling of the walls closing in, not being able to breathe, and wanting to jump out of her skin.

Through her description of a panic attack I vicariously experienced to a small degree what it must feel like. Then I remembered a trip to the dentist when I had to have a crown replaced. I had been given several injections to numb the area. The shots contained epinephrine, which apparently I'm very sensitive to, and my heart started to race.

Then they put protective eyewear on me that had tiny little pinprick holes in them, through which I could barely see, and all of a sudden it felt as though the walls had closed in. Finally, they put a bite guard into my mouth and I felt as though my jaw had locked up and so I started to choke. I began to feel panicky and I ripped off the glasses. I couldn't control my breathing. Luckily my dentist is really great so he made sure I was feeling comfortable before continuing, and all I could think was, "Did I just experience my first panic attack?" That minor occurrence, that thankfully hasn't reoccurred, is a drop in the bucket compared to my friend's description of what she goes through.

It's the same with depression. I've had bouts of feeling sad and blue when relationships have ended and have felt unmotivated, wanting to crawl into bed and stay there, snuggling with my dogs and self-medicating with red wine and chocolate. But those times quickly pass and don't interfere with my everyday life as it does for someone who suffers from clinical depression. When I feel a bit blue in the short, dark days of winter it can't be compared to someone who suffers from serious, chronic depression. Yet I know that my small insights into anxiety and depression have given me empathy and compassion for those who do suffer.

As Sonja Lyubomirsky writes in *The How of Happiness: A New Approach to Getting the Life You Want* that "many experts believe that depression has a become an epidemic. By some estimates, clinical depression is ten times more likely to torment us now than it did a century ago. Several forces may be behind this development. First, our expectations about what our lives should be like are greater than ever before . . . Second, *our increasingly individualistic culture leaves us all alone to manage our everyday stresses and problems, compelling us to blame only ourselves for our shortcomings and failures* . . . And perhaps most important may be the unraveling of the social fabric. Compared with previous generations, we feel far less belonging and commitment to our families and communities and are thus less buffered by social support and strong meaningful connections to others."

In fact, a 2014 survey by Globoforce showed that having friends at work makes a tremendous difference in an employee's workplace happiness and engagement. Those meaningful connections at work help to increase company loyalty and help employees trust leadership more. It also helps improve employee engagement and gives employees emotional support. Therefore, seeking out companies that have a more tribal culture can dramatically improve your mental health by providing much-needed support in today's fractured society.

For Reflection

What do you see as the pros and cons of a tribal culture? An individualistic culture? Which one do you feel currently dominates your life?

CHAPTER 22

Communication Through a Trust-Based vs. Fear-Based Lens

"Communication through interaction is less about the words spoken than it is about the interaction dynamics that take place at the nonverbal level; it is at this level that trust is established—or not."

—*Judith E. Glaser*

There are generally two types of people: those who are open to trusting someone immediately, and those who aren't open to trusting and need time before they trust someone. I tend to be the former, easily trusting others until they might break that trust. I don't think either way is right or wrong, it's just our natural tendency (like being an introvert or an extrovert), but how trust plays out in the workplace is crucial.

In every workshop I have facilitated for a team, the group eventually concludes that communication is a key element in working well with others. Miscommunication is responsible for a lot of the conflicts and issues in organizations. Miscommunication can affect employee morale and also contributes to employee errors. With so much weighing on good communication, why is it that we don't focus on teaching good communication skills to our children? Communication is a SKILL so we know that it can be learned. There are some simple and basic communication principles that if implemented would enhance communication. And that's why the fourth phase in my Tribal Abundance program is about communication.

Good communication definitely helps to create trust and it also enables trust to be deepened. When someone does what they say they will do and follows through on their word, we know we can trust them.

When people communicate with one another from a place of trust and authenticity, rather than fear, there is a desire to really listen to, and an increased understanding of, one another.

The concept of Conversational Intelligence® (C-IQ) developed by Dr. Judith Glaser in the book of the same name, provides a framework and a set of best practices for the way individuals, teams, and organizations listen, engage, build, and influence each moment and shape the future, in all situations. When we use our C-IQ in business, we strengthen the organization's culture to achieve greater business results.

As Dr. Judith Glaser shares in her book, "When we are out to win at all costs, we operate out of the part of the primitive brain called the amygdala. This part is hardwired with the well-developed instincts of fight, flight, freeze, or appease that have evolved over millions of years. When we feel threatened, the amygdala activates the immediate impulses that ensure we survive. Our brains lock down and we are no longer open to influence."

For example, having our ideas attacked in a meeting or being dressed down by the boss triggers our brain's fight-or-flight response and we may react in ways that are not in our best interests. When we operate from that fight-or-flight response state on a consistent and regular basis, we actually do damage to our physical and psychological selves; in fact, even our ability to build our memories is negatively affected.

And when people focus their attention on their fears, they activate their fear-based neural networks and process reality through a fear-based lens. For example, one might be focusing their attention on a loss of approval, and thus the neurochemistry of fear kicks in and they become unable to process reality through a trust-based lens.

Most of us join companies with the aspiration to do well, to contribute, and to bring value. We all want to be successful, respected, and admired by our colleagues and bosses. When we fail to perform, we get embarrassed, or are fearful of looking bad, we may resort to our most primitive behaviors.

Research indicates that when we are comfortable with someone, our heartbeat becomes more coherent, sending signals to the brain to relax, open up, and share with that person. On the other hand, when we are *not* comfortable with someone, our heartbeats may be more erratic, and then the neural signals the heart sends to the brain inhibit higher cognitive functions. In order to practice C-IQ it's important to be aware of how we react in times of stress. By being self-aware and recognizing when we are in a fight-or-flight response, we can adjust how we react and prevent ourselves from viewing reality through the fear-based lens. Adjusting can be as simple as counting to ten, taking some deep breaths, or walking away from the situation.

A crucial conversation, as defined by the authors in the book of the same name, is one in which 1) opinions differ 2) the stakes are high and 3) emotions are high. If these types of conversations are handled well, break*throughs* can occur, and if they're not handled well, they can lead to break*downs*. It's no surprise that the authors believe that whole relationships can hinge upon how these conversations are dealt with. Having open, honest, authentic communication is foundational to building trust and learning how to have difficult conversations. It is a skill set definitely worth learning.

After the authors of *Crucial Conversations* conducted several studies of communities, they found that it was not necessarily those with the most *problems* which were dysfunctional. Instead, dysfunctional communities seem to be that way because they deal with the issues inappropriately. Communities that embraced the issues and discussed them in open honest dialogue were "healthier" than those who either tried to control or ignore them. If the dysfunctional communities were to implement a C-IQ skill set, it is likely they would become much "healthier" in their communication.

Another great book about how to have difficult conversations is *Fierce Conversations: Achieving Success at Work and in Life, One Conversation at a Time* by Susan Scott. She shares seven principles of fierce conversations.

Her first principle is: *master the courage to interrogate reality.* Examining the reality of the world around us it makes me think about the way we all have stories playing like movies in our heads. In those movies everyone is playing a part and we determine the motives behind everyone's behavior. But no one can get into our heads to watch that movie with us, so if we don't verbally *share* our reality with others they have no way of knowing what it is we're thinking.

Her second principle is: *come out from behind yourself into the conversation and make it real.* Having real conversations can feel scary because we feel vulnerable having them. So, we stuff down what we're really thinking and feeling and therefore don't say what we really want to say. We have "unreal" conversations. But once you take the plunge and commit to openness and honesty, you will crave the real conversations and the thought of having any other kind just won't feel right.

Be here, prepared to be nowhere else is the third principle. Have you ever had a conversation with someone who said, "Uh huh, uh huh, uh huh," almost robotically and you could tell it was because they had been told that acknowledgement was the sign of a good listener? You could see their eyes shifting around and focusing on you intermittently and you felt as though you could say anything and they would still say, "Uh huh, uh huh, uh huh," because they weren't really listening? Contrast that to someone who makes eye contact, who focuses on what you're saying, who asks clarifying questions and reflects back what they heard you say. In the latter scenario, you definitely feel as though what you're saying is important to them. This is how you want others to feel as you apply this principle.

The fourth principle is: *tackle your toughest challenge today.* This is very much in alignment with Tribal Abundance and reminds me of the bible verse in Ephesians 4:26 that says "Do not let the sun go down while you are still angry." Address those issues and don't let things fester.

The fifth principle is: *obey your instincts.* How often have you heard someone say, "Go with your gut," when it comes to making a decision? That's because our instincts have been picking up on all that we've ever learned (and what our current reality is) and we are synthesizing that in an unconscious way. The definition of intuition is "the ability to understand something immediately, without the need for conscious reasoning." One of the challenges I face in my coach training is allowing my intuition to guide me, putting my brain on pause and thus not overthinking. We become so used to relying on facts and figures and our five senses that we often don't allow our intuition to guide us. But the more you start tapping into your intuition the more in tune with it you will become. And then allowing it to guide you, obeying your instincts, will become second nature.

Take responsibility for your emotional wake is the sixth principle. The concept that the conversation IS the relationship seems obvious but it's strange how often people forget that. The language that is used is important and we have to be conscious of our words. The concept of "being impeccable with your word" from *The Four Agreements* is an excellent example of this principle. I've noticed that when I am careful with my words and craft a message that takes the other person's perspective into consideration, then I can convey almost any message, no matter how difficult the situation may be.

The final principle of *Fierce Conversations: Achieving Success at Work and in Life, One Conversation at a Time* is *let silence do the heavy lifting.* Some conversations seem to be a race, where everyone is jumping in to make sure their voice is heard and there is no silence.

And yet, without a little time for thought and reflection in a conversation it's difficult for insight to develop. Allow yourself to pause a little and rise above the cacophony of sound that often passes for communication.

For Reflection

Which of Scott's seven principles do you find the most difficult to follow? And which do you think you have "in the bag?" What strategies have you used to support yourself when in fight-or-flight mode?

CHAPTER 23

T – Taking Stock and Building a Tribe

"Measurement is the first step that leads to control and eventually to improvement. If you can't measure something, you can't understand it. If you can't understand it, you can't control it. If you can't control it, you can't improve it."

—*H. James Harrington*

Prior to the existence of Tribal Abundance, I worked in an organization that had a fairly low Tribal Abundance Quotient. The Tribal Abundance Quotient is a measure based on a self-assessment I developed to help individuals and teams identify how much of an abundance mindset they have and how "tribal" they are. For this particular organization I worked in, it was all about scarcity and competition. People were pitted against one another. There was a need to one-up others, to not show any weakness. I was the evaluator on a week-long training course at one point, and I sat through it observing, making notes, and working to capture ways that the course could be improved. At the end of the course I conducted a focus group without the instructors present to get some honest feedback on what went well and what didn't go so well.

After I gathered all the data, I was in the process of writing the report when I got an email from one of the attendees. She asked me to send her my notes from the focus group. This participant was the administrative assistant for one of the federal employees who had oversight of the training facility. I worked for the government contractor that reported to him.

It is highly irregular for an attendee to request that type of information, and as an evaluator I wanted to honor the promise of confidentiality and be in alignment with ethical professional conduct. My gut was telling me that she somehow wanted to use this information to further her own agenda. So I emailed her back and said that it was not policy to release the raw data but that I would be delighted to share a copy of the final evaluation report with her.

The proverbial shit hit the fan; she complained to her boss because she didn't get what she wanted, he then then took it up with my manager's boss, and then he came to me in a flutter about the situation. I stuck to my guns and appealed to his knowledge of ethics in evaluation to explain my response to her email. It became clear that it was my use of the word "policy" in the email—being in such a policy-driven environment— that was apparently such a major faux-pas.

It was another Lucy Moment. I hadn't done anything wrong. I was trying to uphold the ethical standards of the evaluation I had conducted, and yet somehow, I was in trouble. I can remember the feeling of bitterness rising in my throat, almost feeling as though I might throw up, and then the tight, squeezing feeling in my gut. My anger grew and I started to shake...I was so furious with the person who had started all of this drama. I visualized confronting her, yelling at her and cutting her to shreds verbally, and it made me feel a little better, but I knew there was nothing I could do. I was in an environment where it was either kill or be killed and I didn't have the heart to commit murder. There was nothing tribal at that workplace.

The first phase of the Tribal Abundance program, Taking Stock and Building a Tribe, is about getting started and identifying your, your team's, or your company's Tribal Abundance Quotient. Like the quote by H. James Harrington at the beginning of this chapter implies, it is important to take stock and measure where you're at before you can figure out where to go next. His perspective comes from a productivity/quality and continuous improvement perspective and so the word "control" is about the manufacturing process and not necessarily about people. Clearly, it's not about controlling people, it's about identifying your starting point so that you can measure the ways in which you are making progress.

The Tribal Abundance Quotient provides that starting point, by helping you to identify the following: how aligned with scarcity versus abundance are you? How aligned with scarcity versus abundance is your team? Your company? This assessment gives a snapshot of how tribal a group is at the beginning of the journey. (Please see Appendix A to take the Tribal Abundance Quotient Questionnaire. You can also access the online version for individuals at www.tribalabundance.com.)

There is freedom in letting go and not worrying about what you control, what you have, what you lack, and that strong desire to have more. Sometimes there is a need to fill the aching, gaping hole inside. And I understand the rush to fill it, when you feel you can completely disregard the needs of others and their desires because you MUST fill this hole.

But, if you can trust that once you release that desire and look at the emptiness, you can then acknowledge that you can allow the room, the space, for it to be filled positively. Like a beautiful meadow in the wilderness that is filled with blooming wildflowers, allow that hole to be filled naturally because there truly is enough. And without you getting in the way and scrambling to fill the hole, these "flowers" will have room to grow, to sway in the wind, to nourish you, and to spread naturally.

Your Tribal Abundance Quotient helps you to identify those areas in which you are still held a prisoner. It helps clarify your thinking about the areas of your life in which you operate from a scarcity perspective.

Be brutally honest with yourself. We often respond to questions about ourselves based on how we think we SHOULD respond or perhaps how we would like to. Try to think of specific examples from your past and make your responses based on them. Self-awareness, seeing ourselves as we really are, is the first step in embracing a life of Tribal Abundance. Without self-awareness we cannot uncover those parts of ourselves that are hidden, that are dirty, that are ugly. It takes a lot of courage to dig deep and reveal those things because in showing our vulnerability we can be hurt, we can be disappointed, we can be betrayed. Yet without taking that risk, we stand to lose it all, to continue on in our life of "comfortable" mediocrity, lying to ourselves about the truth of who we are and what we desire, numbing ourselves with habits and compulsions and addictions that keep us prisoner. It's as though we are blindfolded and have the power to remove the blindfold but choose not to because we are afraid of what we will see.

Many times in the past have I been disgusted by the ugliness that bubbles up in my own heart. I, too, have had selfish thoughts when I thought, "This is MINE!" and didn't want to share, whether it was regarding an idea, a client, or a project. And I also had those envious thoughts that seeped into my mind when I compared myself to someone else.

One day, a friend and I were leaving a workshop that we had co-facilitated together. During our drive we discussed the workshop and how it had gone. It had been tough. We had several participants who didn't want to be there, and one in particular who was overtly antagonistic. Our workshop was about mentoring—the participants were all mentors—and at one point we had them all close their eyes and follow instructions as we guided them to fold a piece of paper in various ways. Not having the ability to gather feedback from non-verbal cues (as their eyes were closed), the shapes everyone ended up with were wildly different from everyone else's and from the shape the facilitator had directed them verbally to fold. This exercise is a simple yet effective tool to open up discussions about communication and interpersonal relationships and how we can each perceive things differently. In a group of self-aware adults, the debrief discussion afterwards is powerful and there are usually lots of learning moments.

This particular day, I was the observer and my colleague led the activity. When she asked everyone to open their eyes and hold up their paper, one participant was noticeably angry and frustrated. He expressed those emotions by telling us that he didn't think much of the exercise and began to complain about it and how it "should" have been done. He was frustrated that he hadn't been able to get it "right" because the instructions weren't clear.

Therefore, he missed the point entirely. It wasn't about creating the perfect shape that exactly matched that of the facilitator's, it was about the experience and how that could be applied to being a mentor and interacting with a mentee, and how important it was to understand how easy it is to *mis*understand another's words.

My colleague handled it beautifully, taking a coaching approach to his frustration and asking him questions like, "What about the activity was frustrating for you?" and then reframing his responses so they applied to the mentoring relationship.

But that didn't seem to be enough for him. He wanted us to admit that it was an activity without clear directions. His brows were furrowed and I could tell he was clenching his teeth. He wasn't going to budge an inch and he wanted us to know that. His stiff posture and the way he separated himself from the rest of the group clearly communicated that he thought the workshop was a waste of time.

When we had split the room into pairs earlier, the person we had paired him with refused to partner with him. After an awkward silence someone stepped up and said they would be his partner. He was in the group, yet not a part of it, and I observed how this rigidity kept him from being accepted. He was someone that did not seem to be liked, and curiosity had me wondering how he had come to that place. How does someone end up being the person everyone loves to hate?

Rather than letting him derail the whole workshop we agreed to disagree and moved on. We acknowledged his frustration with the activity and then we invited him to move onto the next part of the workshop with us, letting him know that we needed to stay on schedule but that we would both be happy to discuss it further with him at the end of the workshop. (He didn't take us up on that.)

My question to you is, how well do you do when you don't have a lot of guidance and direction? How do you react when things are ambiguous and don't make sense to you? Do you react like the workshop participant did, with anger and frustration, wanting to pin the blame on someone? Or, do you react with curiosity? Do you dig a little deeper and wonder what's going on at a deeper level? This is the first crucial step for someone who wants to create a culture of abundance.

The first phase of the Tribal Abundance program, Taking Stock and Building a Tribe, is about helping a team of people to have a shared understanding of themselves and one another. The assessment tool I use is called PRINT® and it helps to reveal the unconscious motivations that drive a person's behavior and actions.

(For more information about PRINT®, please visit The Paul Hertz Group at https://www.paulhertzgroup.com/.) I have found PRINT® to be an incredible tool for teams who wish to better understand one another and to help them begin to work towards building a tribe.

There are many other assessments and tools out there that can be used for this element of Taking Stock and Building a Tribe. The key piece is to help individuals gain a greater understanding of themselves, and then increase their understanding of others. The goal is to provide a framework that will help people to explain to themselves and others why they behave the way they do. It's also important to have some tools and strategies in place so that people continue to behave as the best version of themselves while at work.

For Reflection

What does it mean to you to take stock?

CHAPTER 24

R - Rapport

"You want to work with people who you like
and have an easy rapport with."

—*Mike White*

walk into a room full of strangers and introduce myself. I see many friendly faces and naturally gravitate to the woman who smiles at me warmly. I sit next to her and strike up a conversation. We're at a baby shower, so we begin talking about the guest of honor whom we both know and the delightful changes soon to come into her life. We connect easily, flowing from one topic to the next with the ease of old friends. Even though we've just met, there is a natural rapport between us.

This type of easy rapport is the foundation of the second phase in the Tribal Abundance program. It's about first identifying any scarcity behavior and then co-creating a new way to behave and interact.

Releasing that need to fill the "hole," and coming to the awareness that *there is no hole to fill* is so important. By taking off the blindfold and looking past what *is,* all the possibilities that exist and can *be* become limitless. Release that need to grasp everything for yourself. Even if you don't recognize that it's what you are doing, every time you push past someone, step on someone, feel that burning feeling rise within your chest because you want to declare, "Mine!" you are allowing a fear-based scarcity mindset to have control. You allow that false image of the gaping hole within yourself to lead you, without realizing that the release of that image, the release of the belief of lack, brings you more than you can ever imagine.

It's like a song bird who is caged, lives a comfortable life and does not realize there is a wide world out there: the beautiful trees and bird companions that would enrich its life. There is so much more beyond the gilded cage around your heart.

When I read *The Four Agreements* by Don Miguel Ruiz, I was so struck by the simplicity of the agreements and how they can help shift one's perspective.

The Four Agreements are:

1. Be Impeccable with your Word
2. Don't Take Anything Personally
3. Don't Make Assumptions
4. Always Do Your Best

The second agreement is the one that is most powerful to me, to never take things personally. I remember joking with my roommate, Alida, about how I took everything as a compliment. We were living in Budapest, Hungary, and had come the serve the church. We both felt as though we were following the call of Christ and wanted to make an impact on the world. Our days were filled with meeting with women in the church, hosting bible studies, and participating in outreach activities. For me, this was a return "home," although I had never lived in Hungary before. As you now know, all my relatives on my father's side were there and my heart was there, too.

In all the challenges and struggles of day-to-day living and being in full-time ministry, I had the powerful ability to stay positive and cheerful. I remember sharing my personal philosophy with Alida of how I took everything as a compliment. Even when someone said something negative or spoke a thinly veiled insult, I took it as a compliment.

"If someone insults me, of course it's really a compliment because obviously they're jealous of me and are trying to tear me down to feel better about themselves!" I laughed. It was a philosophy I had developed almost by necessity, a way to protect myself from the unkind words of others, yet it had somehow become a part of me, flowing through me like my blood and filling me with a confidence that helped to balance out all my insecurities and fears.

This is what resonated with me as I read that second agreement. I worked hard to not take anything personally, reframing everything into a compliment, no matter how challenging that could be at times, and somehow by a wonderful accident—or divine inspiration—I gave myself the tools to navigate the murky and often turbulent waters of life.

In addition to implementing *The Four Agreements*, in order for your team (or for you, if you're working on your own) to complete this phase of Tribal Abundance, focus first on identifying any scarcity behavior. You can use the framework of the Tribal Abundance Quotient to dig a little deeper. Where did the team score highly? Where did it not score as well? What are the areas in which the team might be displaying scarcity behavior?

Once you have identified areas of scarcity behavior, you can work together to co-create a new way to behave and interact. You can use the Tribal Abundance Quotient as a framework and spend some time together as a team reflecting on *how*, and *in what ways*, the people on your team:

- Are generous
- Appreciate others
- Choose to be around positive people
- Choose to see opportunity each day
- Focus on what they have, not on what they don't have
- Foster collaboration
- Foster win-win situations
- Give to others
- Know that there is more than enough
- Look at loss as an opportunity
- Share with others
- Trust others
- Use positive words in conversations
- Work through issues

Look at those areas where your team did not score well and consider making those priorities for your team. Brainstorm on how you can incorporate more of the behaviors listed from the exercise above into your everyday work life. Make the behaviors simple and actionable so that there are clear expectations and mutual agreement. And remember, don't try to change *all* the behaviors *all at once!* Prioritize just a few ideas for the one to two areas where your team really needs to focus. Celebrate the areas in which you are currently successful and things are going well, and commit to maintaining and strengthening those areas.

I worked with a team that recognized there were some issues around trust. The team was a fairly high-performing team in that they made timely decisions, people were engaged, and for the most part there was openness and honesty in communication. Yet, while having a discussion during a workshop on managing conflict, they began to see that they did not completely trust one another. This lack of trust meant that some team members hesitated when giving their opinions as they did not think they would be listened to, nor did they believe that their input would be considered valuable. The team had not completely established rapport to the point where feelings and ideas were understood and communicated well.

The team worked together to come up with some solutions. In a facilitated session the team decided that in order to build trust they needed to be more open and honest in their communication. They brainstormed different ways in which they could do this and came up with a list of behaviors to follow. This included respectful listening, which is in alignment with the principle of *Be here, prepared to be nowhere else* discussed earlier. Also on their list was giving everyone a voice, and ensuring that each team member had a chance to provide their input into decision-making that affected the team.

Once the team had come up with the list of behaviors and discussed what it looked like to put them into action, they crafted specific language to use when they needed to have difficult conversations. They decided that the phrase, "Would you be open to some feedback?" was a non-threatening way to introduce a conversation in which there might be differences of opinion. They agreed that when this language was used they would override their egos and focus on respectful listening. As they put this behavior into practice they reported back to me that the trust level had increased and that those team members who had felt reluctant to give their opinions now felt more comfortable in doing so.

We'll talk more about implementing in the next chapter.

For Reflection

How do you think rapport can be created?

CHAPTER 25

I - Implement

"It's important to have a sound idea, but the really important thing is the implementation."

—*Wilbur Ross*

The next phase, one of the most challenging steps, is to *implement* your ideas: implement a new code of conduct, a new way of engaging with one another that is based on an abundance mindset.

Throughout my career and in running my business, I have always been surprised when others don't follow through: that person who told you they would send you an article via email and yet they never did, the person hired specifically to create something and they just didn't do it, or that person who promised they'd be there for you and yet weren't around when you needed them most.

A lack of follow-through, a lack of implementation, feels wrong. And that's why this step is so important in the process. If you don't put the new behavior into practice nothing will change…you and your organization will stay exactly where you are, continue doing exactly what you've been doing, and therefore will have exactly the same results.

This is the Just Do It phase of the program. And this is where I find goal-setting and coaching incredibly valuable. When it comes time to implement the Tribal Abundance program's principles and learning, start with baby steps, small actionable items that you can easily incorporate into your daily and weekly practices.

What exactly are we implementing? If your team has completed the exercises in the previous chapters, then you have calculated your Tribal Abundance Quotient and have identified areas where your team might have a scarcity mindset. You then used the Tribal Abundance Quotient to identify areas where your team wants to grow in its abundance mindset and made a list of behaviors that will help you to develop rapport among the team. You are beginning to co-create a new way to behave and interact. The implementation piece is crucial; how many times have you begun an initiative and not followed through? How often has your team gotten excited about an idea, project, or program, yet abandoned it without implementing it fully? Once you commit to taking action, *hold one another accountable and stay the course.*

When I'm working with a team, individuals come up with the action steps they want to see the team take and therefore they are able to hold one another accountable. As the team's coach and facilitator, I check in with the leader and team members to see how they're doing. I love seeing the different ways that teams come up with to help one another follow through and stay the course. Sometimes it's posters and signs, other times I've seen pictures and objects used to remind people. Checking in during team meetings is a great way to stay on track.

One of the teams I worked with had identified "foster collaborations" as an area in which they had a scarcity mindset. While overall the team's tribal abundance quotient was high, this was an area they identified as one in which they wanted to grow. They brainstormed a list of behaviors on a flipchart to help them develop rapport; there were quite a few behaviors that they listed, but one of the behaviors that resonated for everyone and was chosen as a priority was to put themselves in others' shoes when interacting. The idea was that in order to foster collaboration they needed to focus on understanding the perspective of others.

Once they had their prioritized list they talked about ways they could implement the behaviors and hold one another accountable. This was where they got to be creative and have fun! There were lots of ideas flowing and they ended up creating signs which read, "Remember the Platinum Rule!" to help remind people to step into others' shoes when interacting, to see the other person's perspective to increase understanding. Because the signs were posted in very public places they were not only great reminders but also enabled great accountability. This helped them implement their idea and the transformation in the team was powerful. The team found that it was fostering collaborations with greater frequency and those collaborations were helping to build relationships among team members.

It can be more of a challenge when it comes to implementation as an individual. Perhaps as you've been reading this book you've recognized that you want to start shifting from a scarcity to an abundance mindset. And perhaps you've identified that you are going to use positive affirmations to help you make this shift. It's important that you not only set a very specific goal (and even better, make it a SMART goal—**S**pecific, **M**easurable, **A**ctionable, **R**ealistic, **T**imebound) and that you write that goal down. Then find accountability. Make sure you ask someone to keep you accountable by checking in with them regularly to let them know how you're doing on meeting your goal(s).

For Reflection

How can you hold yourself accountable as you implement? And how does this link to holding yourself accountable for your own perceptions?

CHAPTER 26

B - Blind Spots

"Everyone has blind spots, and even the
brightest people are no exceptions."

—*Li Lu*

Fair warning: this chapter has a lot of information.
Buckle in and see which concepts resonate with you
the most, and if you can, take the time to examine them
in your life or do some further research via the books
I have referenced.

My husband has a newer vehicle and one of the
features that I am most impressed with is the blind
spot detector. When he is driving and puts his blinker
on to change lanes, his vehicle warns him if someone

is in his blind spot. I have an older vehicle and don't have this feature, and I have to be vigilant not to be lazy about looking in my blind spot when I change lanes. I've had it happen more often than I'd like to admit that sometimes I don't check because I *think* my blind spot is clear. I may have checked my blind spot earlier and so I think it's okay to change lanes. The sound of a horn blaring alerts me to the fact that it was *not* clear and that someone must have driven into my blind spot without me noticing. That's why it's called a blind spot.

We all have blind spots in our lives; there are things that we *just don't see.* I read an interesting article once on EthicalSystems.org about the concept of blind spots and how they affect our ethical decision-making. The article talks about how it's easier for us to "see" the ethical failings of others more clearly than we see our own. We have blind spots any time there is a gap between what we see and what actually is, and when it comes to making decisions it explains why we make unethical decisions without being conscious of it. One of the most poignant examples of ethical blind spots in decision making is the Challenger disaster that happened in 1986. This tragedy has been scrutinized and dissected and there have been numerous case studies published discussing the ethical issues.

The space shuttle Challenger disintegrated in midair on January 28th, 1986, sending six astronauts and a schoolteacher, Christie McAullife, plunging into the Atlantic Ocean. This tragedy overwhelmed us in the United States and I still remember walking through the student union building at the University of New Mexico and seeing everyone glued to the televisions throughout the building, completely captivated by the news reports. We couldn't believe it had happened.

The book, aptly named *Blind Spots*, by Professor Max Bazerman of Harvard Business School, identifies the blind spot that allowed political and managerial considerations, rather than the ethical considerations of the lives of the crew, to drive the decision-making. He states that this was not necessarily a conscious decision; he believes people's emotional needs can drown out ethical considerations completely and that our ethical lapses are usually unconscious. We all have blind spots. In the next phase of the Tribal Abundance program we focus on identifying the conversational blind spots we have while we're implementing our goals. We then collaboratively determine some abundance-based communication styles to help address these areas.

Our brains are amazing things, fearfully and won-derfully made. It's the job of our brain to protect us from harm and keep us safe. It enlists the whole body in doing its job, and when you experience conflict, tension, bullying, or frustration, your brain sends a mix of hormones to your body, as we covered in Chapter 22, telling it to FIGHT or FLEE. It wants you to be safe and the amygdala, the very core of your brain, hijacks all thought and reason. You can feel your pulse race, your face flush, perhaps you tremble and your mouth goes dry. You are poised to react to protect yourself.

Ironically, that very reaction is exactly what will keep you from saying or doing something that will *benefit you* in most situations. That strong urge to react would be so much more appropriate in a world where you were facing down a saber-toothed tiger or where a marauding tribe attacked your village, plundering and taking you captive. In today's world, while we may often face very real dangers, the need to fight or flee in a conversation—no matter how difficult, no matter how painful—no longer serves us. And add to that the cognitive distortions we have or even the conversational blind spots that Dr. Judith Glaser lists in her book *Conversational Intelligence*, and it's a wonder that we have any productive communication at all!

As a team, it's important to identify those blind spots and to find new ways in which to communicate.

I've certainly experienced each and every one of these blind spots we need to be aware of them in order to communicate effectively. Dr. Glaser lists five blind spots in her book and I'll focus on four of these. The first blind spot of *assuming everyone thinks like me* is tricky as it almost seems like common sense to acknowledge that, "Yes, of course people think differently than I do!" but in practice it's so very easy to assume that others are understanding and agreeing with what you are saying.

The second blind spot of *feelings change our reality* has to do with the emotional aspect of a conversation. Think of a time when you've been in a conversation and for whatever reason you become really angry or frustrated, or experience some other strong emotion. All of a sudden, you're not rational and how you interpret the conversation is through the filter of your emotion. Your feelings have changed your reality and you've got a huge blind spot in your conversation…you've likely stopped hearing or understanding what the other person is trying to say.

The third blind spot of *I remember, therefore I know,* has to do with how we think we remember a conversation and what someone else said, yet often what we're actually remembering is what *we think* about what someone else said. The fourth blind spot, *I am listening so I actually know what you really mean,* has to do with where the meaning of the conversation resides. We often think that when we are saying something, that the meaning of what we are saying is in our words. However, the meaning of the conversation actually resides in the listener. They are hearing what we say, yet everything is filtered through their experiences and their memories. They are going to make meaning from what we say based on that filter.

You can see how these blind spots might get us into trouble in our conversations. Unfortunately, unlike the car example, we don't have a device to tell us when something is in our blind spot! And that's not all. Our cognitive distortions can also become blind spots, and like having blind spots in decision-making or communication, these are ways that our brains can lie to us. One of the tools I share with coaching clients when appropriate is a handout titled *Cognitive Distortions, How we distort our experiences.* This is a list of the ten top cognitive distortions that can become blind spots in our lives that was adapted from Dr. David Burns's *Feeling Good Handbook.* There are many more cognitive distortions but I'll focus only on the four that I see most frequently when working with teams.

The first cognitive distortion that can become a blind spot is *discounting the positive*. This happens when we acknowledge that something positive has happened, yet reject it by discounting it. For example, when you get praise for doing something well you might discount it by saying, "Well, the only reason he praised me for that is because he feels guilty for not having done it himself." You basically insist that your positive achievements or actions don't count.

Another one I see is the cognitive distortion of the *shoulds*. This is an easy one to pick up in conversations with someone because you hear the words, "should," "have to," or "need to" over and over. This is about using guilt as a motivator and while we know that it may seem to be a great motivator, in reality it is a *horrible* way to do so because we end up feeling miserable and resentful. I still remember my mentor telling me, "Ildi, don't *'should'* all over yourself!" and the double entendre cracked me up. It's also a great way for me to remember this cognitive distortion and help me to keep it from becoming a blind spot in my life.

The distortion of *labeling* happens when we attach a negative label to ourselves or others or overgeneralize something based on one instance or experience. This distortion may show up as the inner critic ("I didn't get it done; I'm a complete failure.") or as a blanket statement ("He is *always* late," after one instance of being late).

If you take everything personally or feel as though you are to blame for everything you may be experiencing the *blame & personalization* distortion which often goes hand-in-hand with the *labeling* distortion in my experience.

I was working on a program evaluation for a non-profit client, and my colleague and I were sitting in a small conference room with the executive director and the program director. We were discussing the scope of the project, how we could help, and what specifically they needed from us. And then all of a sudden, the executive director made a disparaging remark to the pro-gram director. The program director responded in kind with harsh words and a defiant attitude. I'm pretty sure my mouth dropped open in surprise. I couldn't believe that two professionals—two people who were serving in a nonprofit organization to make the world a better place—were acting like children having a fight. I froze. I had no idea what the appropriate response was. So I ignored their argument. I just kept going, pretending that nothing was out of the ordinary.

Later, when I was thinking about the event, I realized

that the two of them had dispensed with civility and politeness to one another a long time ago. They had become so used to this pattern of interacting that they didn't even think twice about behaving badly in front of others.

What's it like in your organization? Do you find that people try to be civil to one another, or have they given up?

There are some basic principles in communicating with others that help to keep conversations from deteriorating to the point that I experienced with those clients. I like to think of these principles as abundance-based communication styles. An abundance-based communication style is one in which there is no fear, no scarcity, no worry that someone else will "win" in the conversation.

"People don't listen." Yes, you've heard it a million times and yet you KNOW that you're a good listener. It's those "other people" that aren't good listeners!

I'd like to challenge you to focus on listening more in your next conversation, and to try to complete these steps:

- Listen
- Reflect back
- Probe for understanding

Did you notice that there's nothing in this approach about YOU and what your needs are? That's because it's not about you, it's not about you getting your say or winning an argument, it's about listening to the other person to understand *their* needs. You'll get a chance to have your say, but that's not your primary goal here.

Keep the conversational blind spots we discussed earlier in mind, because it's so easy to fall back into old patterns of behavior, especially around communication. These blind spots are called exactly that for a reason. How easy it is to become lazy and forget to check your blind spot when passing or changing lanes! You only have to have one near-miss to get your heart racing and the sound of blood pounding in your ears to remind you to check your blind spots.

It only takes one heated argument in which voices are raised and hurtful words are said to get you to remember to check those conversational blind spots. Just as we have to be attentive when driving to be aware of our blind spots and avoid a crash, be aware of these potential conversational and cognitive distortion blind spots and be diligent in recognizing them.

For Reflection

Which of the conversational blind spots or cognitive distortion blind spots resonate for you?

CHAPTER 27

A - Abundance, Encouragement, and Gratitude

"The key to abundance is meeting limited circumstances with unlimited thoughts."

—*Marianne Williamson*

The next phase of the Tribal Abundance program is about abundance. We've discussed the concept of abundance and given many examples of how to begin to shift from a scarcity mindset, but how do we actually make a shift to abundance-based communication styles? How do we shift the way we communicate so that we are coming from an abundance mindset rather than one of scarcity? How can an abundance mindset become part of our everyday thinking, an almost unconscious part of us?

You've already taken the first few steps in the previous three chapters. Shifting your mindset—and therefore the way you communicate—to one of abundance starts with behaving *as if* you already have an abundance mindset. As you have identified you or your team's areas of scarcity mentality, begun to develop rapport through evaluating how you interact with others, started to implement different ways of behavior, and thought about the blind spots that might be holding you back, you have already begun to make a shift in your mindset. It's almost difficult to separate out this step from the others as your behavior naturally starts to change. And yet, focusing specifically on this piece is important so that your mindset supports all the steps you are taking to move towards Tribal Abundance.

I can remember thinking about how we don't encourage one another enough as humans, and trying to figure out what the root cause of that is. Encouraging others doesn't take anything away from you. I don't know how the belief came about that we need to withhold encouragement from others when they do well. It's as though somehow, we think that praising someone who has done well will give them a big head and then they'll be arrogant and unbearable, so perhaps we think we should nip it in the bud. And thus, we don't give that much-needed encouragement.

Or maybe we think that if we encourage someone who did something well shows poorly on us because maybe we didn't do quite as well and perhaps there's even a little envy or jealousy involved. And thus, we don't give that encouragement.

Yet I believe that we NEED to give that encouragement, we NEED to tell others how well they're doing, how much we admire them, how important they are to us. It's crucial to recognize that encouraging someone *isn't going to take something away from* us or diminish us in any way.

Closely linked to this is: why don't we give one another the recognition we all crave? Perhaps you don't give someone else the appreciation they deserve because you crave it for yourself. You've worked hard and accomplished a lot too, after all, and why should someone else get all the acknowledgement? But the ironic thing is that the more you withhold recognition from others, the less likely it is that you'll receive it yourself. Conversely, if you give recognition and encouragement to others on a consistent basis, you'll soon find that they begin to recognize and acknowledge you as well. Abundance is key here!

I can remember when I was first taught about the concept of spiritual gifts. The one gift that others told me I had—and that I also acknowledged seemed to fit me really well—was the gift of giving encouragement. I thought about how good I felt when I had the opportunity to encourage someone; it filled me with such lightness and joy. The word "encourage" means to give support, confidence, or hope to someone, and this seems to be a natural ability I have. Using this is fulfilling for me and makes me feel connected to others…it is natural for me to practice the spiritual gift of giving encouragement.

I choose to practice encouragement in my professional and academic circles as well. In committing to encourage others I soon saw that people were thirsty for it and that it wasn't something that seemed to naturally occur among colleagues and classmates. Somehow, the more I encouraged others, the more they began to encourage me, although I certainly wasn't doing it in order to get it in return. It just seemed to be the natural response from others, and then the more encouragement I received the more I wanted to give. It was a positive cyclical effect and it felt as though I was rising higher and higher on a cloud of love and goodwill.

Shifting to an abundance mindset includes changing how we communicate with others; we can acknowledge, recognize, give credit to, and encourage others. And we do it, not because we want them to do the same for us, but because it feels good and gives us an opportunity to bring something positive into the lives of others.

Finally, as you focus on shifting your mindset it would be remiss of me to not include the practice of gratitude. One of the leading researchers on gratitude, Dr. Robert Emmons, has studied the effects of gratitude on physical health, on psychological well-being, and on relationships with others. The physical, psychological, and social benefits of simply keeping a gratitude journal are irrefutable. For my own gratitude practice I use a journal called *The Five-Minute Journal* by Intelligent Change. The journal gives a structure for a morning routine that helps you set a positive tone for the day by asking three simple questions with a focus on gratitude. Then at night there is a routine to reflect on the good that happened during the day—again, focusing you on gratitude—and that guides thinking about ways to improve. All this in five minutes a day!

Remember that a mindset is simply a belief, a mental attitude or inclination, that is not fixed. It can be changed. You have the power and ability to begin making the shift from scarcity to abundance; cultivating an attitude of gratitude is a great way to get started. There are a lot of other techniques that can be used such as positive affirmation, EFT (tapping), and cognitive behavior therapy. The key is to acknowledge that your mindset needs to shift, and then to choose one thing you will commit to doing consistently. Take each step in the Tribal Abundance process and allow each step to build on the next step. You've got this!

For Reflection

In what ways do you practice gratitude?

CHAPTER 28

L – Legacy

"A people without the knowledge of their
past history, origin and culture is like a tree
without roots."

—*Marcus Garvey*

Just as we can rewrite the narrative of our own personal lives, a company can rewrite the narrative of its mission and how to live that out. The final phase in the Tribal Abundance program is about creating a legacy together. This happens when the organization or team develops new company rules collaboratively and, if appropriate, a new company mission is written. For those who feel that the word "rule" is too restrictive and scarcity-based, consider thinking of it in terms of a code of conduct. Now that your team has agreed that it wants to work together and interact in a different way, how can you formalize that so that there is a documented agreement that you can refer to, that holds you accountable, and that can be used to onboard new employees (integrate new employees into an organization) and share with them the way the team or organization has agreed to work together? It's also important to keep checking in to see how you're doing.

An exciting way to solidify the new agreement together (mission statement, or code of conduct) is to take part in an organizational philanthropic project. Whether it be building a house through Habitat for Humanity, feeding the homeless, visiting senior citizens, or planting an urban garden, it's important to reach out *together* to solidify the work of the tribe. This provides team members an opportunity to practice some of the concepts they've learned. And as an added bonus, research has shown that volunteering provides individual health benefits in addition to social engagement. Volunteering and helping others out benefit us just as much, if not more so, than those we are helping.

Not only is your team leaving a legacy of good works, it is leaving a legacy of what you have accomplished.

The legacy includes the documentation of the process you went through, the list of behaviors you have agreed to change, the listing of the blind spots your team has identified, the ways in which you hold yourselves accountable, and the new team, organizational, or company charter (or code of conduct), and possibly even a new mission statement. A legacy is something that is handed down from the past, and there is an almost innate desire in us as humans to leave a legacy. Think of the stories your grandparents and parents told, sharing about your family history—that's a legacy. We also leave a legacy in the way we are stewards of this earth and how we manage natural resources; what kind of legacy are we leaving for future generations? This concept of leaving a legacy is vital when it comes to our workplace culture and how we can create a positive and lasting change. Think about the ways that you can pass on the legacy of all that you have learned and how you can positively impact future generations.

It was through one of the online learning courses I took, during a period when I was very focused on building my business, that I first heard the phrase "A rising tide lifts all boats." It resonated so deeply with me because I felt as though it perfectly expressed my belief in supporting others and collaborating with them instead of competing.

It feels as though I have been on a tide that continues to rise over the past several years. I have friends and colleagues who are pushing themselves to be better, to do more, to make an impact in the world and to enjoy success. And the more I spend time with these like-minded people, the more we encourage one another and aim higher. We are working together to leave a positive legacy in the world of work. The tide is definitely rising!

For Reflection

What are some ways that you can leave a legacy?

THE PRACTICE

CHAPTER 29

Battle of the Mind

"You have power over your mind—not outside events. Realize this, and you will find strength."

—*Marcus Aurelius*

I think one of the toughest things about being an entrepreneur is the constant almost daily battle of the mind. If you're not careful—heck, even if you are—there's a bombardment of thoughts and inner voices that say things like, "You're not good enough," "You're never going to succeed," "Who do you think you are?" and "What makes you think you're so special?"

It's never-ending. Those voices can wear you down, make you want to throw in the towel and quit. I'd be lying if I said I didn't think about giving it all up and taking on a "normal" full-time position. Sometimes it's a struggle to keep those thoughts at bay.

During my coach training, I learned about those inner voices and how to deal with them. Whether you call them limiting beliefs, the inner critic, or gremlins, they are voices that we've heard at some point in our lives that make us question what we are doing. They typically come from our childhoods when well-meaning people used those words to protect us in some way from fear, failure, or hurt. Somehow those words stay with us when they no longer have value, they hang out in our brains and show up at the most inappropriate times to make us question ourselves, question our abilities, question the very goals and dreams we have for our lives.

I'd finished developing my Tribal Abundance program and I knew what I needed to do next—reach out and share my program with potential clients—but I was frozen. My inner critic was having a heyday. I couldn't seem to stop all the negative and doubting voices that were resounding in my head. It was as though I had been filled with quick-drying cement and I could not move. Not only did I feel frozen…I was stuck. And I was stuck in a big way. I felt paralyzed and unable to take the first step of coming up with a list of prospective clients. And so I just ignored it all and hoped it would all go away somehow. It felt too scary and I didn't care that I had spent hours and hours and poured my heart and soul into a program that I believed would be life-changing and transformational. I just gave up. The program still existed, but my passion and excitement slowly ebbed away until all that was left was a dull ache of a broken promise to myself, a breath, a shadow, a lost hope of what might have been.

I was busy with consulting and coaching work, although I really wanted my Tribal Abundance program to be my main focus. The first step was to conquer the inner critic, to mute the voices that told me no one would be interested, that I wasn't well-known enough for Tribal Abundance to be a success and that there was nothing new and exciting about my program anyway.

While I've written about EFT (tapping) as a tool for managing the inner critic, another effective technique for quieting those voices is to identify the voice and then name it. You could give it a name like "Ildi's Evil Twin" or even a cartoon character's name, and then when you hear that voice again you can talk to that persona and let them know that their perspective is not wanted. Sounds a bit kooky, yes? But it's an effective way to personify those voices and then thwart them.

So, when I was feeling so stuck, I dug down deep and identified the voice that I kept hearing. It's the voice I call "Ildi the Perfectionist." You can probably relate because perfectionism seems to be a common limitation. Once I recognized and acknowledged that Ildi the Perfectionist had taken over, I was able to talk to her and let her know that I no longer needed her. It felt very freeing to say, "Look, I know that you have worked very hard because you have high standards, but I don't need you anymore. I don't need to have impossibly high standards and I don't need you to keep me stuck. Please leave and I don't want to hear from you again." And then I was ready to move on.

For Reflection

What are some ways that you strengthen your mind?

CHAPTER 30

Going Home

"Where we love is home—home that our feet
may leave, but not our hearts."

—*Oliver Wendell Holmes, Sr.*

I went back to Hungary to visit my family in 2016; it was thirty years since my grandfather had passed away. My cousin had driven me to Nógrádsipek, to show me the plaque honoring my grandfather for the twenty years he had spent as the Catholic school's director. We had brought flowers, but the gate to the school was closed and locked.

When the current director finally came and opened the gate, she also showed us the apple trees behind the school that my grandfather planted. He was a beekeeper and he brought his skills to the area where many people still kept bees and supplemented their incomes with the money they made from selling honey. My grandfather passed on some of the bees to my cousin, who now has someone taking care of them. He's busy running his company but talks about someday taking care of the bees in his retirement. It's a way to honor our grandfather.

The bees love the apple blossoms so I'm sure that's part of the reason my grandfather planted them. As we looked at the trees—old, gnarled apple trees, growing halfway up the hill—I felt connected to him. He lives on here, not only through the apple trees, but through the lives of the people he taught.

The plaque was beautiful. It was displayed on the wall of the school that faces the street. The photo of my grandfather was one from when he was young, around the time he first started teaching in the school. He was a handsome man with strong features and a commanding presence. As I gazed at his photo and read the words honoring his life, memories started to flow. I remembered the man who paid us one *fillér* (less than a penny) for each fly that we killed (the pig in my grandparents' neighbor's yard brought a lot of flies around), the man who gave me a shot of *pálinka* (apricot brandy) that he had made and how he grinned when I almost choked on the liquid fire pouring down my throat. I remembered also the man who made me *kakaó* (hot chocolate) as a special treat for my breakfast during the time in Hungary when buying food was a challenge. I remembered my grandfather's love, I could feel the warmth and happiness I experienced in his presence, and I could almost hear the sound of his voice saying my name.

"You're his favorite!" my father had told me, and whether or not that was true, I felt like the most special person in the world to him. Because my two brothers and I were the only of his grandchildren who lived far away, the time he spent with us was precious to him. He had four children and fourteen grandchildren—thirteen after his first grandchild, my cousin Jutka, passed away at the age of sixteen—and he loved us all with a kind of love that was deepened and strengthened through the experience of being tortured in a prisoner of war (POW) camp. I felt that his experience of being tortured—something he never talked about—opened up in him the ability to love even more deeply. He had the amazing ability to forgive and let go, and move on with a great capacity for love and forgiveness. It reminds me of one of my favorite quotes by Kahlil Gibran, author of *The Prophet:* "Your joy can fill you only as deeply as your sorrow has carved you."

As I stared at the plaque, I was reminded of the kind of man my grandfather was, and how his strong faith and principles shaped his children and grandchildren, and how it will impact generations to follow. I felt connected to him in a very visceral and real way.

And as we left Nógrádsipek and drove through the beautiful Hungarian countryside, I gazed out window as we drove back to Balassagyarmat, reflecting upon how powerful the experience had been. On the way, we stopped at a little coffee shop, Café Frei, in Szécsény where we sat and had cappuccinos and pastry. The day had been one of strong emotions and I was glad for a chance to catch my breath, relax, and enjoy the company of my cousins before I headed back to Budapest.

I share this story of my trip with you because to me it perfectly illustrates how, no matter where we are, where we live, or how often we see them, we are always connected to our tribe. And I count myself lucky to have family members who are also part of my tribe.

Reflection

Who are the members of your tribe? How do you stay con-nected with them?

CHAPTER 31

Connection

"People crave comfort, people crave
connection, people crave community."

—*Marianne Williamson*

It feels as though the driving question throughout my
life has been, WHY? Why do people behave the way
they do? What makes people react in a certain way? Why
do certain things bother some people and not others?

That incessant curiosity is why the principles described
in Dr. Stephen R. Covey's book, *The 7 Habits of Highly
Effective People* resonate with me so deeply, especially the
principle of *seek first to understand, then to be understood.*
If I can seek to understand others, then I am able to better

understand myself. It's a principle for successful living, and I am proud to say that it's how I've been trying to live my life for many years. And in that curiosity, that drive to understand others, some of the other life principles that I've gathered over the years through my experiences are: don't compare, we can change our thoughts, we have power over our emotions, and we are all connected. The fusion of these philosophies is the foundation of the overall Tribal Abundance philosophy. Tribal Abundance is based on the concepts that we are all connected, we are members of tribes, and that there is enough, there is an abundance, and we can collaborate in our tribes and not compete. It's about trusting people and reflecting that trust in the way we communicate with them.

Imagine if you had a work team in which you felt connected, people operated with an abundance mentality, there was collaboration, trust, support, and open, honest communication. How much more would you enjoy the people you work with and the job you do if this were your reality? I work in a team like this and it's amazing the difference it makes. We identify as a high performing team and truly live this connected piece as we interact with one another and accomplish great things for our clients. There isn't any masterful manipulation happening in the background because we are all committed to one another and to our team. It doesn't mean that the team is perfect or that there are never any issues—that just wouldn't be realistic for a team of imperfect human beings. Yet, there is a commitment to working together so that the team is successful. This is the difference Tribal Abundance makes and being in that type of environment allows each one of us to flourish.

Remembering how important encouragement is, this is my encouragement to you: begin to implement the principles of Tribal Abundance into your life, begin to live in accordance with this philosophy. You will notice how things will begin to shift, you'll notice how you begin to transform and leave behind those thoughts, habits, and behaviors that no longer serve you. And you will begin to see the wonder in what others are doing and to acknowledge those actions.

Writing this book has been one of the most powerful experiences I've had: allowing my emotions and thoughts to just flow is cathartic and as I discover my voice I become more of who I truly am. Connecting with that place deep inside me that has stored up all the joys, hurts, pain, happiness, love, and memories has brought me such a sense of relief. I'm sold on the whole concept of being a writer, sharing my story, allowing my voice to speak. And yet, even this experience has not been something I've done on my own. From the friends who encouraged me to pick up a pen to start writing, to the writing coach who helped me find my voice; from the editor who refined my language and pushed me to express myself more clearly, to the book publicist who found the nuggets of gold in what I'd written; from the publisher who saw the potential in my manuscript and embraced me into her circle, to the readers who have encouraged me with their feedback. My tribe has gathered around me for this book and we have accomplished this together.

And as I write this I see that word "allow" in the previous paragraph and it tells me that I've stifled this in the past in my hurry to resolve things, learn, grow, and keep moving. In the past, I've given myself short shrift in the area of reflection. While I've always been curious about "why," now my voice strongly declares the WHY without worrying about analyzing, dissecting, or picking apart everything to find solutions and answers. It just is, and my voice is like an aria, rising to the heavens.

For Reflection

What is your biggest insight from what you've read so far?

CHAPTER 32

The Opposite of Separation

A warm feeling flowing throughout my body. Sensing that there are others out there like me and not like me, and we are all together, all focused on making it on this pulsing, spinning, crazy ball of earth and water that is a mere speck of dust in an infinite galaxy.

Having a stranger smile at me and open a door for me as I'm walking into a building— that warm feeling spreads and encircles me like a hug and then flows out and connects me to others. It's like a wave in the ocean that splashes over me gently and pulls me with it into the warm embrace of the water.

The water carries me and I'm bathed in the light touch of water surrounding me and caressing my body with its gentle touch while I feel the warmth of the sun as I float. As I float I remember Lucy, I see her face and want to reach out to her.

It's funny how it's in the completely random, unexpected times of my life that Lucy revisits me. I see her round, smiling face and think about the times we played together as children. Without even knowing it, I've held onto Lucy throughout my life. Sometimes the memories surface and I think about where I've traveled, the life journey I've been on, and how she has always been with me, even if I'm not always conscious of her.

In a place of Tribal Abundance, we don't want to ignore or suppress painful memories. It's about acknowledging them, voicing them, and then allowing the resulting healing and growth to happen. It makes me think of a physical wound on a body: you acknowledge the pain, you clean the wound, and you allow it to heal. Once it's healed, you may have a scar, but that scar reminds you of how you got the wound so you don't repeat the mistake and injure yourself again. The scar doesn't hurt, it simply serves as a reminder that you were hurt in the past.

That scar on my heart that has to do with the wound of the end of my friendship with Lucy doesn't hurt any longer, but it does remind me that she is somehow with me and that humans are precious and need connection, and no matter how different we look on the outside, we are all the same human race. We may decide to befriend someone based on something superficial, yet once we peer past the surface and come to know a person for who they truly are, we connect with what's really important. What is important is connecting and allowing that connection to help us learn and grow and to be better people.

When it comes to how we may heal those wounds, we have many options. After acknowledging that we have let the hurt go, we have to make a conscious decision that whatever it was that happened no longer has any power to harm us. Part of that step involves forgiveness; whether it's forgiving yourself or forgiving others, this is an essential part of letting the past go. You may want to reach out to a counselor or therapist to support you in this step.

Once you have worked through the letting go and forgiveness phase, the focus shifts to cultivating new thought patterns and new ways of thinking. In Sonja Lyubomirsky's book *The How of Happiness: A New Approach to Getting the Life You Want,* she suggests several strategies for practicing gratitude and positive thinking. One of the exercises she references is journaling about your best possible future self. This is an incredibly helpful exercise; in fact, journaling has many positive benefits including clarifying your thinking and helping you to solve problems more effectively. One of my favorite journaling practices is writing my Morning Pages (three pages of stream of consciousness writing) which is an exercise from Julia Cameron's book *The Artist's Way.* When I start my morning with this practice it helps me to clear my mind, get focused for the day, and work through any issues that I may have. There are many other mindfulness and meditation practices that you can incorporate to cultivate new ways of thinking and to help you grow and develop as a person.

For Reflection

What are the experiences you've had that have had the strongest influence on who you are today? What are some practices you follow to support your personal growth?

CHAPTER 33

Learning to Trust

"Whoever is careless with the truth in small matters cannot be trusted with important matters."

—*Albert Einstein*

I had such a strong desire to do a good job and help my team succeed when I worked at the training company. Yet, I felt thwarted and constrained at every turn. Working as a contractor meant that there were many rules and regulations to follow, and they kept changing all the time. It created uncertainty in me and it caused me to lose trust in my natural instincts and intuition about what was right. There was an atmosphere, maybe even a culture, of trying to find mistakes so that they could be corrected. When the focus is always on what might be wrong, it creates a culture of mistrust and "pointing fingers." If something is wrong, then "someone must be to blame." And of course, no one wants to be blamed for doing something wrong so they've got to defend themselves, protect themselves, and learn to build a case as though they were on trial for a crime they didn't commit. The amount of stress this causes is tremendous, and of course it erodes trust because no one has any idea who is on their side. Someone might betray their trust because they would rather another person be blamed than themselves.

It was a huge mess and a culture of mistrust and defensiveness had been created over time. There were incredibly smart, creative, talented people working there, yet rather than collaborating and creating something amazing together, they were pitted against one another or left the organization because of the stress and dysfunction.

What's sad is this isn't an isolated case. In my work with organizations, I've seen this many times and it all comes down to the issue of trust. Rather than having a culture where people trust one another and operate in Tribal Abundance, they lack trust and it hampers them and keeps them from being their best. No matter how much team building an organization does, without a foundation of trust they'll never achieve what they want to.

Research shows that when we are open and trusting we have better communication. And better communication in turn builds trust. But I think the key word is "open;" when we trust we are more likely to be the best version of ourselves. When there is a lack of trust we close up, we become less likely to communicate well, and we also shut down our creativity and our best ideas. When we're in a state of mistrust it is hard for us to be the best version of ourselves. Also, when we trust others there's less chance that we'll take things personally. We believe the best of others and this shows up in the way we communicate and how we interact. There is a sense of peace and calm in an environment that is built on trust, while in one in which there is no trust there is an underlying tension. That tension is palpable in an environment of mistrust and creates blocks between people. In Tribal Abundance, you naturally work on building trust with others.

If you are interested in learning more about the topic of trust, there are many amazing books out there. One of my favorites is Patrick Lencioni's *The 5 Dysfunctions of a Team* because I really appreciate his approach through storytelling. There's something compelling about a good story and the fables he writes are effective at helping to get the message across. It's important to highlight the importance of trust because without it, managers or leaders are fighting a losing battle.

For Reflection

How do you view trust? What is its role in your workplace relationships?

CHAPTER 34

Bringing It Home

"Gratitude is one of the strongest and most transformative states of being. It shifts your perspective from lack to abundance and allows you to focus on the good in your life, which in turn pulls more goodness into your reality."

—*Jen Sincero*

When an organization focuses too much on the culture of individualism, it manifests in the mindset and behavior of its people. Employees' own self-interests prevail, with the costs of deteriorating relationships with colleagues, lack of innovation, and decreasing productivity, which negatively affects the good of the whole. When the focus is on competing rather than collaborating, this downward spiral into difficulty is where you'll go.

There are many companies out there who try to help organizations change their cultures. They tend to work by first identifying the existing culture, visualizing the desired culture, and then they take steps to address the gaps between the two by changing the leadership structure, reorganizing, changing the rules, or incorporating new management tools.

Unfortunately, this process fails to address the core cause of almost all issues: the belief in, and fear of, lack or scarcity—and the behavior that arises from that. If this root issue is not addressed, issues of all kinds will remain or return and no significant permanent change can occur. A scarcity mentality is a recipe for not being able to make a transformational shift.

As we've learned in this book, it really isn't a one-and-done type of situation. To this day I will sometimes find myself operating from a place of scarcity. Whether it's with respect to my time ("But I PAID for a full hour!" when I'm being shorted on a coaching call), or when I am thinking about how I spend my money ("I can't believe I'm spending $5,000 for this business development program—what if it doesn't work?!"), I sometimes slip back into scarcity. Our limiting beliefs pop up at the strangest and most unexpected times, even when we are committed to an abundance mindset. Don't worry, it DOES become more of a habit to stay in abundance and you'll find yourself making the mind shifts quickly and more easily as you continue to be aware of your thoughts. Companies will SURGE in their success by doing what the forest people did. Remember those wonderful BaMbuti?

Have you worked for an organization that chews up and spits out its employees? (Maybe you're still working for that organization?) That feeling of stress, that churning anxiety in your stomach, is a natural reaction as your body tells you, "This is NOT the way to live." Imagine instead a place where:

- you trust there is enough, like the forest people did, and where you will be able to be generous and open to the goodness of the whole.
- you put the tribe's well-being above the individual's, and you enable all employees to do the same, creating a collaborative environment that can take the company to previously unknown heights of success.
- you seek food (abundance) together (tribe), and when you involve everyone in the process of

prosperity, you will experience a culture that is unstoppable in attaining it.

- you create a culture of unrestricted sharing as they did, and you will foster the mentality of abundance…no one will feel as though they are lacking.
- you handle conflict by coming together as a group to resolve issues, not focusing on right or wrong but on restoring peace, and you will create a culture where people are not afraid of conflict and are not afraid to work through issues.
- you create a culture where employees feel an equal collaborative role with the company, where they "sing" to wake it up (i.e., take ownership of its health and success if they see it waning), and you will cultivate an unshakable loyalty within the company, as well as a powerful protection against failure.

Being a part of an organization like this has been life-changing for me. I'm incredibly grateful to be part of a high-performing, positive, collaborative team and never have to worry about how I "come across." We embody all the principles listed above and our team is a dynamic force to be reckoned with. There is such a high level of trust that the concept of ego is almost nonexistent.

Imagine a tribally abundant workplace culture where this is not only possible, it is the new norm!

* * *

I leave you with this letter to Lucy as the loss of our friendship is something that has remained with me all these years and is ultimately what led me on the path to creating Tribal Abundance.

Dear Lucy,

As I write this letter to you an image of you as a child comes to mind. You had beautiful skin, an almost blue-black velvety color, and so your smile looked incredibly bright and white in contrast. You had short curly hair, and I remember us touching one another's hair, marveling at the texture and how different it felt from our own. I remember playing together and the delight we took as young children in the pure, simple joy of just being with another little girl.

Our friendship ended with the birthday party incident, yet you have stayed with me all these years. I have no idea where you went, what your life was like, or even if you're still alive. Our lives were likely very different. My family emigrated to the United States when I was ten—to the land of freedom and opportunity, a land truly flowing with milk and honey—and my guess is that you remained in South Africa. There weren't as many options for you as a black female in apartheid-era South Africa. While there may have been opportunities for you to go to school, your schools would have looked very different from the schools I attended. Not only were they less equipped with fewer teachers, the whole school system was closely identified with the apartheid system and so there was a commitment on the part of young people to destroy the school system. There were strikes and vandalism so it really was not a place to learn and be educated.

It wouldn't be until you were much older, perhaps in your late twenties, that South Africa would begin to experience a shift and the situation around education began to change.

You likely wouldn't have had many opportunities for a career. Most likely you became a domestic worker like your mother. Maybe you got married and had children.

And how would you be able to protect your children from the pain you experienced? I can imagine your face, crumpled up, squeezed into a crying ball of hurt and betrayal. All you wanted was to go to a birthday party—cake! ice cream! balloons! games!—and yet your young-girl's heart was broken by the realization that you were not allowed to attend based on the color of your skin.

Was this your first loss of innocence too? Did your heart break, as mine did, when your very soul screamed, "This is wrong!" but as a child you had no power and no voice? Did you feel helpless, as I did, as those I trusted, the adults in my life, made decisions that wounded me deeply in a way that could never truly heal? Was that the moment when you began to realize that not everything is okay? That the world out there brings pain, hurt, and fear?

Lucy, wherever you are, I want you to know you have always been with me. I've had many Lucy Moments throughout my life and they have helped to shape and transform me into the woman I am today. A woman I am proud to be.

I hope that you have had Ildikó Moments throughout your life as well. And I hope that they are not the moments of pain, betrayal, and rejection that you experienced, but rather that they were the moments when someone embraced you for who you are with the innocence of a small child, when someone opened their heart to you in friendship. I would love it if our story would lead to a change in this world.

With love,
Ildi

My wish for you, dear reader, is that when you face your Lucy Moments you don't become discouraged and give up; instead you are motivated to do better and open your mind to possibilities. Whatever you dream of is within your grasp, especially with your tribe at your side.

Appendix A: Tribal Abundance Quotient Assessment

Assess Yourself.

Directions: Please rate the extent to which you agree with each statement below by checking the appropriate box:

	Strongly Agree	Agree	Disagree	Strongly Disagree
I am generous				
I appreciate others				
I choose to be around positive people				
I choose to see opportunity each day				
I focus on what I have, not on what I don't have				
I foster collaboration				
I foster win-win situations				
I give to others				
I know that there is more than enough				
I look at loss as an opportunity				
I share with others				
I trust others				
I use positive words in conversations				
I work through issues				

Scoring:

Count up the number of checkmarks in each column:				
Multiply that number by the number below it:	4	3	2	1
Write that total in each box:				

Add up the four scores for your grand total: Overall Score: [ ]

What your score means:

If you scored between 47 and 56

Your tribal abundance quotient is **HIGH**

You know what it means to live with an abundance mindset. You choose to view life through a positive lens and see each day as a new opportunity. You don't allow negative circumstances or people to affect your outlook or how you go through life. Joy, contentment, and peace are emotions that are part of your life.

Maintain your abundance mindset by focusing on reflection and spending time with like-minded people.

If you scored between 36 and 46

Your tribal abundance quotient is **MEDIUM HIGH**

You are well on your way to living with an abundance mindset. You may struggle at time with some negative thoughts and feeling discouraged. Your speech is mostly positive and you often encourage others through your speech. Some anxiety or hesitation may be emotions that are still part of your life.

Grow your abundance mindset by focusing on sharing with others.

If you scored between 25 and 35

Your tribal abundance quotient is **MEDIUM**

You are growing in your abundance mindset. You may still have some fear and worry that there isn't enough for everyone. While you are working on making your speech more positive, you may still gossip and make petty remarks about others. You may sometimes struggle with negative thoughts and feeling discouraged. Resentment or bitterness may be emotions that are still part of your life.

Grow your abundance mindset by focusing on appreciating others.

If you scored between 14 and 24

Your tribal abundance quotient is **LOW**

You have a lot of opportunity to grow in your abundance mindset. Right now, you may be living with fear and a belief that there isn't enough to go around for everyone. Your speech may be pessimistic, and include gossiping and saying negative things about other people. Envy or anger may be emotions you are very familiar with.

Grow your abundance mindset by focusing on gratitude. "Count your blessings, not your problems."

Take the online version at tribalabundance.com

Appendix B: What If You Hate Your Job?

If you are in a situation where you are one of the Walking Dead at work (not a zombie in the television series) where your motto is "I hate Mondays!" and you can barely make it through Friday to *finally* get to the weekend, this section is for you.

When you are in a job you hate, there are two options: stick it out, or leave.

If you choose to stick it out, you can change yourself, influence the organization in some positive way, or both.

Change yourself: If you are tired of feeling low-energy and unmotivated about your job and yet you're not quite ready to leave, then focus on changing your attitude and behavior. Many of the tips and examples in this book about shifting your mindset will help you. To start your day in a positive way, create a morning ritual that fills you with joy before going to work (some things to consider including: drinking your cup of coffee/tea at a leisurely pace, taking the time to meditate and/or journal, mirror work with positive statements—yes, talk to yourself in the mirror). Practice gratitude and focus on the positive things that are happening at your workplace. You may have to dig deep to find these, but they are there!

Try to influence change in the organization: After you have made a concerted effort to change yourself, you can shift your focus to fostering positive change. I won't sugarcoat this, it's tough. There is a *lot* to this topic, more than I can cover here, but my first suggestion is this: To influence change you must first model the change you want to see (e.g., open and honest communication). It's no good complaining about your workplace when you want to have a workplace where people focus on the positive and don't complain. Find your tribe, others who want to see a better workplace. Wouldn't it be great to create a grassroots movement that gets the attention of key decision makers?

If you choose to leave, you can:

Find another job: This is a great time to brush up your resume and your LinkedIn profile, begin to attend networking and professional development meetings (if you haven't already been doing so) and perhaps even to connect with a career coach to help you find a great opportunity in an organization with a positive culture. You will also want to practice your interview skills. Looking for a job can be stressful so make sure you reach out to your tribe for support.

Go into business for yourself: maybe you have the entrepreneur gene and you are chomping at the bit to go out on your own. You are part of my tribe! Prepare yourself for what to expect by reading *The E-myth revisited: Why most small businesses don't work and what to do about it* by Michael Gerber. There is also a great Facebook group that is run by a dear friend of mine, Dr. Barbra Portzline, called Create Signature Programs That Sell. It's a great way to connect with like-minded individuals and to get some solid guidance and support.

You may use a combination of these strategies to support yourself. Please know that you are not alone and that there is support out there. There is definitely a tribe of people on this same journey; find them and reach out to them so that you can support one another.

Appendix C: Resources and References

Resources:

TED Talks: https://www.ted.com/talks

- Margaret Heffernan: Forget the pecking order at work
- Adam Grant: Are you a giver or a taker?
- Adam Grant: The surprising habits of original thinkers

The Five-Minute Journal, www.intelligentchange.com

The Why of You powered by PRINT®, www.paulhertzgroup.com/what-is-print/

Books Referenced and Tips For Further Reading:

Bazerman, M. H., & Tenbrunsel, A. E. (2011). *Blind spots: Why we fail to do what's right and what to do about it.* Princeton, N.J.: Princeton University Press.

Burns, D. D. (1981). *Feeling good: The new mood therapy.* New York, N.Y: Penguin Books.

Cameron, J. (2002). *The artist's way: A spiritual path to higher creativity.* New York: J.P. Tarcher/Putnam.

Covey, S. A. (1989). *The seven habits of highly effective people.* New York, USA: Simon & Schuster.

Gibran, K. (1923). *The prophet (A Borzoi Book)*. New York: Alfred A. Knopf.

Glaser, J. E. (2013). *Conversational intelligence*. New York, USA: Routledge.

Grant, A. (2013). *Give and take: Why helping others drives our success*. New York, USA: Viking.

Heffernan, M. (2011). *Willful blindness: Why we ignore the obvious at our peril*. London, UK: Walker Books.

Heffernan, M. (2014). *A bigger prize: How we do better than the competition*. New York, USA: PublicAffairs.

Heffernan, M. (2015). *Beyond measure*. New York, USA: Simon & Schuster/ TED.

Lencioni, P. (2002). *The five dysfunctions of a team: A leadership fable*. San Francisco: Jossey-Bass.

Logan, D; King, J.; and Fischer-Wright, H. (2008). *Tribal leadership: Leveraging natural groups to build a thriving organization*. New York, USA: Harper Business.

Lyubomirsky, S. (2007). *The how of happiness: A new approach to getting the life you want*. New York, USA: Penguin Press.

Patterson, K. (Eds.) (2012). *Crucial conversations: Tools for talking when stakes are high*. New York: McGraw-Hill.

Ruiz, M. (1997). *The four agreements: A practical guide to personal freedom*. San Rafael, Calif.: Amber-Allen Pub.

Scott, S. (2002). *Fierce conversations: Achieving success at work and in life, one conversation at a time*. New York, USA: Berkley Books.

Turnbull, C. M. (1961). *The forest people*. New York, USA: Touchstone.

Turnbull, C. M. (1987). *The mountain people*. New York, USA: Touchstone.

Appendix D: The Tribal Abundance Program

Tribal Abundance is a six-month program that helps leaders create a tribal culture of abundance instead of merely changing the rules or the leadership structure. It is based on the anthropological research conducted by Colin Turnbull who studied the Ik and the BaMbuti tribes. **Tribal Abundance embodies the most successful behaviors and habits of the forest people:**

- It fosters a mindset of abundance and roots out the psychology of scarcity that is destroying companies' cultures.
- It fosters a tribal culture over an individualist culture.
- It institutes collaborative, transparent, trust-inducing processes, as well as processes that enhance generosity among all members of the tribe.
- It institutes a conflict-free zone based on a culture where people come together as a group to resolve issues, not focusing on right or wrong but on restoring peace.

And finally, from a place of Tribal Abundance, companies rewrite culture rules by first addressing "restrictive zones" and communication styles—and by developing a tribal project together.

The Tribal Abundance philosophy is defined as "a state of being, or a culture, in which a group of people that have a shared interest or occupation, and have the common mindset that there is **no shortage of resources** (e.g., ideas, customers, profits) and that **there is enough to go around**. This allows them to be **others-focused** and seek to enrich the lives of people they interact with by **collaborating, sharing, connecting**, and **co-creating** (interacting as a tribe) rather than competing. This cooperative approach **maximizes creativity** and **innovation** and reinforces the 'no shortage' mindset."

Endnotes

1   Emotional Freedom Technique (EFT) is a combination of modern psychological approaches and ancient Chinese acupressure; this widely used technique was developed by Gary Craig in the early 1990s.

2   Latham, A. (2016, May 8). What scarcity and abundance mean to your career. Retrieved from http://www.forbes.com/sites/annlatham/2016/05/08/what-scarcity-and-abundance-mean-to-your-career

ACKNOWLEDGEMENTS

With a thankful and grateful heart, I want to recognize my tribe:

- My biggest fan, my husband, Kevin—I love you.
- My wonderful parents, Kálmán and Barbara, who not only brought me into this world but who have supported and encouraged me throughout my life's journey.
- My two brothers, István and Kálmán, and my sister-in-law, Sue—we don't get to choose our family, yet I know that if given the choice I would most certainly have chosen them!
- My in-laws, Larry and Cheryl, kind, giving people who have wholeheartedly welcomed me into their extended family.
- All of the authors and thought leaders who have influenced my thinking (a small portion noted in the References section). "There is nothing new under the sun" and I hope my work helps to extend the light you've shed on these ideas.

- Lizabeth Phelps, whose high standards, creativity, and exacting attention to detail were instrumental in helping me to create Tribal Abundance.
- Jamie Cox, my amazing editor, who took what I had written and polished it till it SHINED, and did that with humor and grace.
- Aly Meech, who designed the logo for my Tribal Abundance program, and whose concept you'll see carried throughout the book in the chapter headings.
- Lila Romero, the book cover designer who immediately "got" the Tribal Abundance concept and was able to illustrate it in a fresh and creative way for my book cover.
- Chloe Gallaway, who was not only my writing coach, but also my supporter, my encourager, and my soul sister during this whole crazy process of writing a book. I could not have done it without her!
- Penelope Love of Citrine Publishing, who embraced me into her family of writers and brought a truly innovative and tribal approach to the publishing process.

- And my marketing gurus—Denise Cassino, who brought her magic and moxy, and Paige Engle, who brought her sparkle and skills to helping me launch my book.

And finally to all my extended family and friends— I gratefully acknowledge that there are too many of you to recognize individually—former, current, and future clients, mentors, coaches, and colleagues. You are my tribe and I am blessed.

ABOUT THE AUTHOR

Living under a name that translates to "fierce warrior" in Hungarian can send many messages to a young girl transitioning from a host of divergent cultures throughout her life. For Ildikó Oravecz, it meant that success best happens when it is not built alone. Through a profound and colorful past that began in South Africa, followed by part of her life in Hungary and then tiny Socorro, New Mexico, Ildi's greatest philosophies were to listen to your gut, build a culture you believe in, and maintain a posture that promotes further enrichment.

She now translates those life lessons into her Tribal Abundance® program, where the concept of collaboration and connection is taught as a framework for ensuring success through interpersonal networks. She designed the program herself, basing the concepts on the anthropological research of Colin Turnbull, who studied two very different tribes and how their approaches to abundance and scarcity resulted in two very different mindsets, usage of resources, and consequences.

Ildi not only lives by the tenets of paying it forward, but she has proven it to be a legitimate principle through a community network that has repaid her with rewarding civic and volunteer connections. She is an Associate Certified Coach (ACC) as well as a Certified Performance Technologist (CPT). She is the recipient of the International Society for Performance Improvement (ISPI) Award of Excellence for instructional design, and holds a Master's degree in Organizational Learning and Instructional Technologies from the University of New Mexico.

Ildi's gift back to the community is realized through several volunteer activities, including board positions and committee involvement. When not coaching or consulting, she balances her life by digging in her garden and enjoying life from her backyard patio; going for walks with her husband; and tending to two rescue dogs that watch her every move, and a wayward cat that lives on her front porch.

www.HighPerformanceConsulting.com
www.TribalAbundance.com

PUBLISHER'S NOTE

Thank you for reading Ildikó Oravecz's *Tribal Abundance: Living Courageously in an Uncertain World*. If you enjoyed this book, you can support the author by helping others find it. Here are some suggestions for your consideration:

- Write an online customer review wherever books are sold
- Gift this book to family and friends
- Share a photo of the book on social media and tag #TribalAbundance
- Bring in Ildikó Oravecz as a speaker for your business, club, or organization
- Suggest Tribal Abundance to your local book club
- For order inquiries, contact Citrine Publishing at (828) 585-7030 or Publisher@CitrinePublishing.com
- Connect with Ildikó Oravecz at TribalAbundance.com

Made in the USA
Middletown, DE
10 January 2020

82984600R00159